Tom Vickers/Todd Seligman © 2008

Hooking Up with Tila Tequila

A Guide to Love, Fame, Happiness, Success, and Being the Life of the Party

Tila Tequila with Sarah Tomlinson

Scribner
New York London Toronto Sydney

Scribner
A Division of Simon & Schuster, Inc.
1230 Avenue of the Americas
New York, NY 10020

First Scribner hardcover edition December 2008

SCRIBNER and design are registered trademarks of The Gale Group, Inc., used under license by Simon & Schuster, Inc., the publisher of this work.

For information about special discounts for bulk purchases, please contact Simon & Schuster Special Sales at 1-800-456-6798 or business@simonandschuster.com.

Designed by Joel Avirom and Jason Snyder

Manufactured in the United States of America

1 3 5 7 9 10 8 6 4 2

Library of Congress Cataloging-in-Publication Data
Tequila, Tila.
Hooking up with Tila Tequila : a guide to love, fame, happiness, success, and being the life of the party /
Tila Tequila ; with Sarah Tomlinson.
    p.   cm.
1. Tequila, Tila. 2. Television personalities—United
States—Biography. I. Tomlinson, Sarah. II. Title.
PN1992.4.T35A3 2008
791.4502′8092—dc22   2008034021
[B]

ISBN-13: 978-1-4391-0153-7
ISBN-10: 1-4391-0153-1

Contents

Intro

FUCK OFF. That's right. I know what you're thinking: Tila Tequila wrote a book? What does that bitch have to say? Can she even fucking write?!

Well, *APPARENTLY* I can. I mean, I write blogs all the time, don't I? And someone's reading them, right? I've only got something like three MILLION friends on MySpace. That equals a whole lot of fans . . . and stalkers . . . plus plenty of secret admirers, too, who I'm sure are taking a great deal of sick, guilty pleasure in logging on to keep up with what I've got to say. I'm tired of giving that shit away for free. So buy my book, bitch!

Alright, alright, don't get all mad. I'm just telling it like it is. I know a lot of people have always thought of me as an obnoxious, slutty bimbo. Not only do I know it . . . I've learned to embrace it and use it to my advantage. Because while everyone thought I was just hanging out at my house, practicing my pole dancing, I've been building an *EMPIRE*.

I can hear you all being like, "I still don't know what the hell she does." Well, for one thing, I'm a fucking author. Yes, *DARLING*, an author! Doesn't that sound intelligent? You can add it to my long list of accomplishments: model, actress, musician, clothing designer, reality television star, Internet maven, humanitarian, and survivor.

SURVIVOR. That last one makes me the most proud. Because it was the hardest to come by, and really, it's the foundation on which I built everything else. This aggro way I have of talking, of telling people to shut the fuck up when they hate on me . . . it's not the real me. It's just one part of me. It's the front I had to put up during all the years when I was busting my ass, pulling myself up from nothing to finally be someone.

And not just anyone. But someone with her own TV show, *A Shot at Love with Tila Tequila* . . . someone *Time* magazine called the Madonna of MySpace . . . someone who's been on the cover of *Stuff*, *Blender*, and *King* magazines . . . someone who's been on Hot Lists in *Rolling Stone* and *Maxim* . . . and best of all, someone who actually feels confident enough to let people get close to her.

This confidence is a new development. It means I can finally relax enough to share my story and encourage my fans to be true to themselves while tearing ass down the path to following their dreams. The whole point of my book is to introduce the real person behind that crazy **TILA TEQUILA** image. I also want to give you some advice based on the things I've realized during my own struggle, so maybe you won't have to learn things the HARD way, like I did.

The Hardest Fight of All

My whole life, I've been fighting. Literally. Getting into fistfights, street fighting, and fighting verbally for everything I believed. Being four-foot-eleven didn't help. I seriously think I've got

little man's syndrome! My shitty childhood didn't help either. And I've always had the kind of dreams that don't just get handed to you. Everything was a battle in my life, to the point where I felt like if I wasn't fighting, there must be something wrong.

But then the craziest thing happened. I got my television show. And the first season, I had this amazing and totally terrifying experience. I have this rule that if I'm going to do something I have to do it **ALL THE WAY**. So I dared myself to really open up to people for the first time ever. And as if that wasn't scary enough, I did it in front of millions of viewers. And it took that show, on top of all I had learned during the years I was working to get there, to help me start relinquishing my need to be tough.

Well, alright, I'm *STILL* tough. And strong. But now I'm tough and strong in so many new and different ways. On the show, there were people who had a lot of serious problems. And they'd come to me, really distraught, to talk about them. I realized, wow, I like this feeling. I want to help people. This finally feels like who I am.

It made me see that I have so much to share with everyone, in the same way I've been sharing my experiences and my passion with my fans on my website and MySpace page for years now. It also gave me the courage to believe I can do the one thing I still value most: find *TRUE LOVE*. I mean *REAL* true love. The *FOREVER* kind.

Top Ten Things You Didn't Know About Me

1 I'm a squirter.

2 I eat at McDonald's at least twice a week. Quarter Pounder with Cheese combo meal, baby!

3 I drink Coca-Cola like Amy Winehouse smokes crack!

4 Lizards and geckos scare the shit out of me! I consider myself a pretty fearless bitch, but put one of these little critters in front of me, and I will cry like a baby!

5 I don't own one single pair of flat shoes. I hate them!

6 For me, driving fast cars is like having good sex.

7 I've had my fair share of fun, sexy rendezvous with a few select famous people, but there is only one famous person who will always top my list. I wanted to marry him, and I still think about him every day.

8 When I was thirteen, I skipped school with some friends. We stole a brown 1988 Toyota Corolla, drove it to the beach, did some donuts, and then dumped the car in the water.

9 When I was seventeen, I used my sister's ID to work at the local strip club after school. Nobody at the strip club knew I was underage.

10 When I was eighteen, I had my very first sugar daddy. He helped me get out of the gutter. I still think of him today, and love him for loving me when no one else did.

The Secret Teachings of Tila Tequila

I not only have my story to share, I have a message, too: Always stay true to yourself.

I know, it sounds kind of cheesy. But believe me, it's the toughest, most badass thing you can do. Because it sure ain't easy. The hardest part, as I can tell you firsthand, is trying to figure out who that self even is.

Take me for example. I've been through a lot in my life, so by now I could probably describe myself as very strong. But that's not all. I'm also smart. I like to have fun. I like to feel sexy, too. But if I had my choice, some days I'd shave off all my hair and go on the red carpet wearing a wife beater, my jeans, and my Chucks.

Being all these different things can be confusing. In this world, people want to label you and try to make you be one thing, just like they want you to declare a major in college and

stick to one career for your whole life. As if. That's so fucking boring!

It's fun to be able to play different roles, to be the elegant woman and the bitch from the street, and even the smart, badass author. If I can do it all, so can you. As long as you know who you are, you can be **ANYTHING** you want.

People have a really hard time with this, though, because often they are hiding from themselves and everyone else. Like on the show, when I went to have home visits, people were like, "She can't come to my house. She can't know where I'm from." And I always felt like saying, "You think this is bad? You should see where I come from."

The truth is, we all came from somewhere. That's the whole point of this book, that it's the stuff from our past that makes us who we are. The hard, shameful stuff doesn't even have to be bad. It's just how you look at it. It can lead to knowledge, which is a gift.

And that's the beauty of it all, isn't it? If I hadn't had so many fuckups in my life, I wouldn't have had the drive to keep moving and to get to somewhere better. Because I'm just like you. I'm not some fucking five-foot-ten Adriana Lima, Gisele-type model. And plenty of people told me I'd never make it as a model or anything else. But I sure as hell did, didn't I? And now that I'm here, I want to pull you up with me. See, I've got this plan for how we can make it fucking awesome for all of us. **NOW** you know what I do.

5

Photos and collage by Kristin Burns

Chapter One:
Sluts

SLUT. Yeah, I've heard it before, more times than I can count. I know they're talking about me. It's nothing new. My whole life . . . as far back as I can remember . . . I've been called a slut. And worse. **MUCH** worse. And do you know what I have to say in return?

Thank you, haters! Thank you to all of the haters who have called me names, and even thought they knew something about me over the years, just because of the way I look. Or the way I dress. Or the fact that I've always been all about doing my own thing and doing it my own way.

It's because of the haters that I'm here today. Their words made me promise myself that I would prove **EVERY** single one of them wrong. Their hate drove me to become a strong, ambitious woman with a successful singing and television career, and millions of fans all over the world. Their hate was the fuel I needed while I was struggling to build all of this from the ground up, with my own hard work, on my own terms.

They can go ahead and call me a slut. I don't care. I'm **WAY** past letting silly little words like that hurt me. And besides, they probably don't even know what it means anyhow. In fact, I'm so beyond getting upset at the haters that I'll even school them on what it really means to be a slut. So here it goes. What exactly is a slut, and how would a person have to dress, act, or be to qualify as one? Well, look it up in the dictionary, and it says:

Slut: (noun) a slovenly or promiscuous woman

Okay, they're saying I'm easy. That just goes to show how little they know. As to getting all riled up about who I choose to hook up with, what gender they may be, or how often I get busy in any given week, I mean, what is this, **HIGH SCHOOL??** Don't they have anything better to do than think about what happens in my bedroom (and anywhere else in my house that I'm feeling on any particular day)? Maybe it's just that they're **JEALOUS**, and they really only talk trash about Tila Tequila because they secretly want to hook up with me. Let me tell you, it would **NOT** be the first time! But please. I've got standards. And I certainly don't waste my skills on haters. Moving on.

If you look up "slut" in a thesaurus, this is what it says:

Slut: She dressed like a slut and didn't act much better. Promiscuous woman, prostitute, whore; (informal) tart, floozy, tramp, hooker, hustler; (dated) scarlet woman, loose woman, hussy, trollop; (archaic) harlot, strumpet, wanton.

You know what? I know those other words, too. Slut is just the beginning. I've been called all of those things, and then some. In fact, if you gave me a crack at it, I could rewrite that thesaurus entry and make it a whole lot longer **AND** a whole **LOT** juicier. I've been called pretty much every horrible thing you could find listed in the dictionary, plus some words that no dictionary will ever print.

But the truth is, those people weren't really talking about my sexuality, or my reputation, or anything to do with any of those things. No. They were talking about my power. Because **THAT'S** what scared them. Even though I didn't have any money, or much of a family, or anyone to fall back on, I had power. Because I didn't care enough about what they thought to want to be like them. Or to be intimidated by them. Or to do what they wanted me to do. And they hated me for that.

They couldn't get free themselves. So it killed them that, even when I was just some eighteen-year-old tomboy, fighting everyone who crossed my path, and trying to find a way out of where I'd come from, I already knew the secret of freedom: Don't listen to anyone except yourself. The haters still thought they could hurt me with words. When they couldn't come up with the right insult or swear word to get at me, they took the easy shot, the cheap shot, and called me a slut.

Working It, Hard

Well, if slut means a young lady who works **HARD** for what she believes in, takes no fucking bullshit from people, stops at nothing to reach all her dreams and goals, picks herself up each time she falls down, believes in herself when no one else does, and inspires other people to never give up on their dreams, no matter how hard life gets, well then, I guess *I AM* a slut. And a proud slut at that . . . thank you very much!!

I got to where I am today on my own terms. I am a self-made entrepreneur, a woman who did everything by and for herself, built a career from nothing, with her smarts, her talent, and her style. And, **YES**, with her looks. I never wanted to be a model in the first place, but I'm not ashamed of the fact that I used modeling to launch my career. It was what I had to make use of right then and there.

I wasn't about to wait around for some record company, or modeling agency, or casting director to tell me I was someone. No way! I made my own destiny, one fan at a time. Was it scary? Fuck yeah! Were there days (and lots of incredibly long nights) during which I wondered when it was going to happen for me? Of course there were. I'm just like you . . . and just like you, I get scared, too.

But did I ever doubt that it would happen for me someday? No way! I knew exactly where I was headed. I didn't need anyone to make it okay for me to want what I wanted or to believe I deserved it. I was never, **EVER**, one to follow other people's stupid, restricting rules! I figured, this is my life, right? Mine and nobody else's. So why should I have to live by rules that were dictated to me by other people, people who have nothing to do with my personal life path? It just never made sense to me.

A Few of My Favorite, Sexiest Things

Sexiest animal: **Siberian tiger**

Sexiest car: **Bentley**

Sexiest beach: **St. Barths**

Sexiest country: **Brazil**

Sexiest body part on women: **Ass**

Sexiest body part on men: **Abs**

Sexiest outfit: **A corset, skinny jeans, and four- to five-inch stilettos. Six inches is like fuck me. Six inches, you're definitely getting laid.**

Sexiest thing in my closet: **Agent Provocateur black corset that's so tight, my waist becomes eighteen inches around. You can't breathe, but it looks fucking awesome. I don't know what you can do in it, but you look hot. Your tits get squashed all the way up to your neck.**

Sexiest beauty product: **Hot pink nail polish and pink glitter lip gloss**

Sexiest beauty secret: **Spray tan**

Sexiest perfume: **Dolce and Gabbana Light Blue. It's worked really well for me. It's gotten me a lot of action.**

Sexiest brand: **Roberto Cavalli. He should hook me up with some clothes ASAP.**

Dare to Be Different

Even when I was a little girl, I knew I was different. Growing up, I never bonded with one group of people. I always had a hard time conforming and trying to *FIT IN*. I was always the loner who felt comfortable hanging out with people of all different races, sexual orientations, and styles. I would find myself wandering back and forth between the different cliques, never totally fitting in any one place, but enjoying everything I learned from all the different types of people I knew.

I might have been alone, but I've never been lonely. Get it? There's a way to be *ALONE* but not lonely, to be *STRONG* but not overbearing. Life and what we make of it is just a balance between everything inside of us and everything in the universe around us. I think finding that balance at a young age has a lot to do with why I've made it this far.

Because you can have the looks, you can have the brains, you can have the talent, and maybe you're even lucky enough to have all of that combined. And it's possible to *STILL* not get anywhere. Because sometimes you need a little extra spark that's not on that list.

I actually liked being alone. It kept me from getting distracted from the things I wanted to accomplish. It made me mysterious. The mystery is what made me powerful. Nobody could figure out who I truly was, or what was on my agenda. That's how I wanted it, because I had a master plan that reached so far beyond where I grew up, or where I went to school, or what people thought of me. If the price for that independence was being called *SLUT*, I was just fine with that.

While they were distracted, calling me names, I was busy drawing up plans for how to take over the world. Muahahhaaha! And look at me now. That early struggle sure paid off, didn't it? So bring it on, bitches!

If people are calling you names, or giving you attitude, it doesn't have to be a horrible, painful thing. It can make you stronger, too. If there is one thing I've learned in life, it's that haters have a huge role in helping you achieve success! So don't ever feel down if people around you are trying to hate on you and make you feel bad about yourself . . . whether they're calling you slut, fag, or any of the other dumb names people with no imagination throw around at the people with *REAL* power who scare them.

Someday you'll come to thank the haters, just like I do. See, had it not been for their horrible name-calling, I don't think I would have ever made it to where I am today! They just made me want to succeed even more, and work all the harder to get there. You might think you want things handed to you on a silver platter, but the problem with that is it won't teach you anything about yourself, or give you that extra ambition and fire you need to move forward in your life! Once you get everything you've ever wanted, you'll have no idea how to appreciate it, or what to do next in your life. Sometimes having it all may actually leave you feeling empty. Sometimes having *NOTHING* gives you everything!

What I'm trying to say is that I know life can be pretty tough out there. I know there are a lot of haters who want to keep you small. But you have a choice to join me and help change the definition of a *SLUT*. Are you going to live by the book, whether it's the dictionary or the stupid rule book that people with no passion want you to live by? Hell, *NO*. This is your world, your life, and so it's your right to live it any way you please.

And you know what? If you really are a slut, according to the actual dictionary definition, then so be it! If you are going to be something, you might as well go all out and be all that you can be, right? Why be half-assed at something? For me, it's all or nothing. Take it or leave it. Love me or leave me. Is that too hard to understand? I didn't think so. Now that you've got it, you can make it happen in your own life, too, you big *SLUT*.

October 26, 2006 2:45 PM
you are the fakest and fucking
lameist peice of shit i have ever seen.
i hope you burn in hell.

Photos and collage by Kristin Burns

Chapter Two: Haters

We need haters. If you don't have one, go hire one. Seriously, dude. Without haters, you'll never amount to anything. They are the driving force behind our success because they make us go, "Oh yeah? I'll show them!" They make us do things we might not have had the courage to do if they'd just kept their hateful mouths shut in the first place. How do you think I got to where I am today? I've had tons of haters my whole life.

Haters are everywhere. But you can't let them get to you. If you hate the haters, you'll just become this person that you hate. And you don't want to be one of those idiots who sits around and talks smack about people, do you? Of course not. You're better than that.

So you have to shut the haters down right from the start. Don't even dignify their bullshit with an answer, or get caught up in a big back-and-forth. It's just that easy. You let them talk their bullshit talk while you walk your awesome, kick-ass walk. Haters just sit around and hate, but you *do*. That's where the power is.

Ignore the Hate

You know, deep down inside, whatever they've got to say is bullshit anyhow. No, really, you do. Alright, I can hear you going, "Sure, Tila, that's easy for you to say now that you've made it big." Are you fucking kidding me? I get more hate NOW than I ever have before. The more successful I become, the worse it gets. Even I get bummed out sometimes by the things the haters say. That's just human nature.

It's up to you to ask yourself why you're listening to them even a little bit. Does it really matter what they think? Are they the people who really matter in your life? No. So why should their opinion count for anything? That's right, it doesn't.

If you're still letting them get you down, then it's time for some tough love. Snap the fuck out of it. Grow some balls. Believe in yourself. You're the only one who can.

Don't Be Your Own Worst Hater

Even if you're luckier than I was, and you get support from your family, they can't feel your feelings for you or think your thoughts. All they can do is say, "You're amazing. The best ever. Don't worry what people say." They can drown out the haters. But at the end of the day, it's all about you and how you see yourself. If you feel like you're not good enough, nobody can change your mind. So don't hate on yourself.

You can use their hate to fuel your fire. Use it to make you a better person. You can even go one step further and embrace the haters. Make them work for you.

That's what I did. My haters said I wasn't pretty enough to model. They said I couldn't sing. So I set out to prove them wrong. I became this really strong girl, and I taught myself how to do things for myself. Because who else was going to do it for me? No one.

The Haters Made Me Do It

My haters really got busy when I started modeling back in Houston. I was a total tomboy as a teenager, and so at first it seemed really weird to put on a bikini and walk around smiling and having my picture taken. The whole idea made me really shy. I was all like, "Oh, you know, I don't think I want to do this. I don't want to get too much attention." I just wanted to do my thing and not stir anyone up.

But then everyone I'd gone to high school with started talking shit about me. They started seeing, wow, this girl is actually trying to do something with her life. She's actually going for it. In true hater fashion, they were like, "Let's break her down so she can't go anywhere. Because we're stuck here in Houston. And if we're not going anywhere, no one else can go anywhere either." It's a vicious cycle.

Before all of this, I used to go out to the clubs and try not to attract too much attention. I'd always gotten plenty of the wrong kind of notice for being a little badass punk anyhow. I didn't want to make it any worse than it already was.

But once I found out that everyone was running their mouths about me, I was all like, "Oh really?! Well, look at me, everyone. I'm the best ever!" It's not even like I believed it back then. How could I? I'd grown up without any love, and so I'd never had any reason to think I was anything special. But I certainly wasn't going to let the haters be right about me being a loser and a failure. They drove me to be the success that I am.

After that, I was like, "If they hate me now, just wait until they see my modeling photos!"

I was on posters for the next modeling expo, and the next thing you know, I was everywhere. I mean everywhere. It was my way of going, "Oh yeah?! Well, here you go then!" Because, as you should know already, if I do something, I really do it . . .

So that pissed them off even more, and they got even louder. They were just saying the meanest things you could say to a person about how I'm short, I'm ugly, I'm a gremlin, I'm trash, I'm a whore. Anything bad you can say about a person, they said about me.

It pissed me off, but it also made me more ambitious. The more people kept telling me that I wasn't good enough, the more I just kept giving them more things to talk about. Because, in the end, they kept talking about me, right? So, all of a sudden, I was the talk of the town, which is kind of ironic, given how much they hated me.

Finally, everyone was talking shit to the point where I'm like, "That's it. I'm moving to Hollywood to live the dream they'd all have if they weren't so scared. Watch."

It was scary. I moved to LA, by myself, with $300. If I'd had the comfort of a real home, instead of nothing but haters back in Houston, maybe I wouldn't have had the balls to do it. But I knew I couldn't turn back because they'd be there to greet me at the airport, going, "We KNEW you'd never make it!"

I wouldn't let them be right about me. Because even if I wasn't as confident then as I am now, I knew I wasn't this bad person they said I was. I knew I had a lot of potential.

Haters, Hollywood-Style

If you really want to get your confidence crushed, Hollywood is the place to do it. But I had already dealt with so much crap in Texas that by the time I moved out here, I wasn't about to get intimidated. At least in Texas, they're Texans. They talk shit, but they're tough. So when I got to LA, and people talked shit, I was like, "Are you serious?" This is the town of hair gel and fake tans. Give me a break!

But it wasn't the haters I had to worry about. I didn't fit in anywhere in LA. Back in the late nineties, there were no acting roles for Asians. Especially Asians with blond hair and tattoos everywhere. I wasn't tall enough to be a fashion model.

I started to lose confidence in myself. Some days I would lie in bed and cry because I didn't think I was going to make it. But that's where my alter ego Jane would come in. My fans already know her. She's one badass bitch. She's the one that's like, "Get the fuck up. Stop feeling sorry for yourself! What the fuck are you going to do, fucking cry?"

So I got up, and I kept working. I realized, just like with the haters, "Who the hell are these people to decide what I'm worth?" So I did it on my own. I built my fan base. It started small but it grew. Then, all of a sudden, the positive happened. It always does.

Haters Always Finish Last

I was only nineteen years old, but I had fans. I no longer had to feed off the haters. My fans were inspired by ME! They were rooting for ME. They were saying, "You can do it for all of us. We're just like you. If you can make it, so can we."

And it's true. You can make it. As long as you stand behind who you are, and what you believe in, and keep working it, the haters will never win.

At that point, I started ignoring the haters. I keep them around, but way in the background, in case I start to feel lazy or forget where I came from. They'll humble me. Because I know they're back in Texas, and everywhere else, talking shit about me on my MySpace page **WHILE** watching my TV show and buying my magazines.

I can go donate five million dollars to Africa tomorrow, and I'll still be a fucking whore in their eyes. But that's okay, because the only reason I've got money to help other people is because of the haters who got me here in the first place. They make the world go round. And honestly, if there's one thing I would hate, it's a world without haters. I'd just walk around feeling complacent and uninspired. And that's just not me!

October 28, 2006 6:43 PM
I want to take you out on a date <3

Photos and collage by Kristin Burns

Chapter Three:
Photos

What? Are you expecting me to get all defensive about the fact that I got my start (and made bank) in a bikini? Nah, I'm comfortable with who I am *and* the fact that plenty of people seem to think I look hot in the buff. This is jerk-off material, plain and simple. So go get some lotion, do what you have to do, and enjoy the next half hour of your life.

Giuliano Bekor

Chapter Four:
Making It

So, did you like that? Did you get your rocks off (or your box off, in the case of the lovely ladies)? Good. I like to keep my fans happy. But that's not the only reason I put so many photos in my book. See, all of these photos, this is how I got started.

The Early Days: The Sky's the Limit

Apparently there's some secret surrounding the path I took to get where I am today. A lot of people have the wrong idea about how it happened. Like I just took my clothes off, and the adulation and money poured down on me like manna from heaven. If only.

I had to work it. That's why I feel so lucky, each and every day, for all that I've accomplished. I've been on my own since I was eleven years old. I've had six near-death experiences. Hell, I'd had my first OD by the time I was sixteen. I wasn't exactly one of those spoiled bitches on *My Super Sweet 16*, right?

I know what it means to hustle. When I got started in the late nineties, people had no idea what the fuck to make of me. A hot Asian chick with blond hair? In *Playboy*? I was all like, "You'd better get ready for this, because I'm here to stay."

Don't Believe the Fairy Tale: How I Really Made It

Back when I was a teenager living in Houston, I had no idea how to make things happen for myself, or even what I wanted to make happen, for that matter. I just remember this feeling of yearning for something more. As much as I loved my hometown, I knew it wasn't the place for me. I needed so much more from my life.

I just knew, somehow, that I had a profound purpose for being here. I wanted to feel truly alive. Being stuck in Houston was the exact opposite. It seemed as if there was just no

way out. I had so many questions: Where do I start? What should I do? Who can I call upon? I didn't have nearly enough answers. So . . . what did I do?

I let my heart lead the way, trusting it fully, without hesitation. My heart was a great guide because I had so many dreams, goals, and wishes, and this feeling in my soul that yearned for something more. Even if that still left me with a lot of questions, I knew wherever this road took me, it was still a hell of a lot better than being here!

From Tomboy to Bikini Babe

I got my first modeling gig when I was eighteen years old. A friend asked me to be one of the models in this local calendar he was putting together. At that time I was quite a tomboy with a reputation as the "Baddest Bitch on the Block." Since I was on my own, it helped if people were a little bit afraid of me.

Modeling and doing other "girly" stuff would ruin my image! I asked all my friends what I should do, and of course, they said it was a bad idea. I was still playing the tough-girl role, so I was like, "Yeah, modeling is so stupid! It's not me! Please!"

My friend really wanted me to model for his calendar, so he gave me two weeks to change my mind. I kept trying to figure out what to do. What was more important? My reputation as a tough girl or following my heart, which told me that this whole modeling thing could be a way out of Houston. And, even better, saying, "I'll do what makes me happy, and whoever doesn't like it can just fuck off!"

Soooo that is exactly what I did! I learned how to grow some balls and be tough in a different way . . . by following my heart. No matter what my friends said, no matter what I thought was right, or safe, or easy, I couldn't deny that my heart really wanted me to try modeling. Even back then, I was starting to see that my heart would always know what was best and push me to go down a different, better path, no matter how scary it was.

The big day for the photo shoot came, and it was fucking weird! I was wearing lingerie, like really pretty, girly stuff. I even had a hair and makeup artist! They did up my hair in soft ringlet curls. I felt so awkward! How does a tomboy know how to "model" in sexy lingerie? I sure as hell didn't.

But the truth is, I'd always known I was a hot bitch underneath the baggy jeans and wife beaters, and so I drew on that confidence and worked it. I just knew, somehow, that this was my chance. I was sure I had potential to be anything I wanted to be, and if this was the first step to getting me there, then I sure as hell was going to make it work.

My friend also ran a local car show, and that's where he premiered the calendar. All of the girls signed autographs. It was my first experience of people wanting their picture taken with me. I was walking around in a bikini thinking, "What the fuck is going on?"

That was my lucky break. I got discovered by a bunch of photographers from California. Modeling still was not my dream. But I did want to get the fuck out of Texas. They paid for my first trip to Los Angeles, and I worked it. I was like, "Hell, yeah, a free trip!"

I didn't care about being a model, but I finally started to admit something I'd known since I was eleven. I wanted to be an entertainer and to be known and admired by millions of people. If this is what I had to do to get my start, I was all over it. Once I made that decision, I never looked back, and never relented, not until I'd made it happen.

I went back to LA to make an appearance at a car show. I was brand-new to the import racing scene, which was huge back then, and I had no idea what the fuck I was doing. All the big-deal, hot-shit car models were all prissy and perfect, and all like, "Oh, no, I don't smoke," in front of their fans. And then, here I come, eighteen, fresh off the bus from Texas. I touch down and go off, just like, "Fuck you, motherfucker!"

I didn't know any better. I was not professional. At all. But it actually worked to my advantage. Everyone was like, "Did you hear that fucking bitch?" Because they couldn't believe it, they wanted to hear more.

Right away, there were Tila lovers. And Tila haters, too. But everyone, and I mean everyone, knew who I was. That's how I liked it then. And that's how I like it now. Love me or hate me, you can't ignore me. And I don't care what you say.

That's the secret to confidence. It has nothing to do with thinking you're better than everyone else or hating on other people. It has nothing to do with other people at all. When you're confident, you don't compare yourself to anybody or worry what they're thinking. You're too busy being kick-ass and making your dreams come true. That's confidence, baby. And you can have it, too. Just stay focused on you, no matter what.

Later that year, I was back in Houston when I got my biggest break of all. I was still eighteen, just walking around the Sharpstown Mall, and what do you know? I got discovered, old-school style, by *Playboy*. I was like, "Hell, yeah, here we go!"

That photo shoot must have gone pretty well because I've been in *Playboy* six times in all. I was their Cyber Girl of the Week in April of 2002, and their first Asian Cyber Girl of the Month. Now I was really getting somewhere. Or at least that's how it seemed.

Fans 'R Us

First, I had to build my fan base. So I put it out there, any way I could, modeling, building my own website, TilasHotSpot.com, and even just every time I went to a club. People who didn't know me, they'd see me, and see how hard I was working it, and how I didn't give a fuck what people thought about me. And they'd say, "There's something special about her. This girl is going somewhere. She's got a personality. I'd like to hang out with her." So they did. They found me online, and we became friends. I shared everything with them, the highs, the lows, the late-night rants and raves, the dreams about being famous someday. And not just because some lame-o executive in a bad suit said I was hot enough, or fuckable enough. They liked me just for being me!

It wasn't like I was conceited about it. After everything I'd been through, I just felt lucky to be alive. And I didn't sugarcoat anything. I wrote about how hard and lonely and overwhelming it could be, too. And how I hated that people could be so totally wrong about me. My fans loved that I didn't hide anything. My life was like a live reality show on the Internet, twenty-four hours a day, way before MTV got a hold of it.

My Internet Adventure

It wasn't just MySpace that made me famous. I've always had a legion of friends on the Internet. It's a paradise for misfits like me (or maybe I should say misfits like us, because I know you've got that badass streak in you, too) who don't fit in anywhere else.

I was already known as Tila Tequila by then. I'd gotten that nickname when I was thirteen, when some friends and I snuck out and started taking shots of tequila. I got sooooo sick! My face swelled up, my eyeballs turned red, I broke out in a rash, and I totally threw up all over the place. That's when I realized I'm allergic to alcohol. All my friends started calling me *TILA TEQUILA*. And it just stuck.

66

But when I was seventeen, my screen name was Tila T Girl. The place to be then was AsianAvenue.com. It was like MySpace, but for Asians. I was so big and caused such a commotion that they kicked my ass off. Fine by me. I wanted bigger and better anyhow.

I found this site called Face the Jury. My name was Kick Azz Girl, and I was the top-rated girl on that site, too. Everyone knew me. After that, it was Friendster. But they kicked me off, too.

Finally, Tom Anderson founded MySpace. He saw that I had an online fan base in need of a home. He wrote to me personally and invited me to join. And so I did. Honestly? It sucked at first. Back then, Friendster was a raging party. And MySpace was a lame party with two people, some deflated helium balloons, and a bowl of stale tortilla chips.

But, as you know by now, no party I'm at can suck for long. I'd already built my own website, TilasHotSpot.com. And I don't just mean I seduced some egghead and got him to do my bidding. I mean I learned HTML and built it with my tiny little hands and my tiny little fan base, and it grew from there. By the time MySpace happened, I had something like fifty thousand people on my mailing list. I mass e-mailed them, and all of my awesome fans followed me. That's how I immediately became the first person to rock MySpace.

67

Living Large in La-La Land

When I was nineteen, I moved to Los Angeles. I had friends who were all about getting head shots, going on auditions, and waiting for someone to give them the modeling job or movie role. I was like, "Fuck that!" I am not going to let someone else tell me how or when it's going to happen for me. Or, more likely, in this town of haters, that it's not going to happen for me because I'm too short, too Asian, or too whatever they decide is out on this particular day. Hell no. I got it together and made it happen for myself.

I was touring around the car show circuit, and that's how I really grew a fan base. At these car shows, there'd be twenty thousand dudes, foaming at the mouth to meet the car show models. They just saw me as a hot poster model in a bikini. But they'd come up to get their picture taken with me and—what do you know?—I'd actually talk back and shit!

They loved that. And they were very loyal. They followed me from car show to car show, and from website to website. I thanked them by keeping it real. And by having the most bumping website out there. It was a membership site (a girl's got to live, right?), so it kept me on my toes. I had to keep them coming back, so I learned how to become a one-stop entertainment superstore. I styled my own photo shoots. I shot and edited my own videos. I made my own calendars, posters, and T-shirts and sold them online. And I kept writing my blog, sharing everything that was happening, and how I felt about it, with my fans. That's how my fans and I developed such a strong bond. And we're still friends.

Things started to take off, but I didn't want to just be a model. That was really just a way to get myself to Los Angeles and generate some excitement for what I was going to do next. I had a plan. I'd kept it a secret because I didn't want people laughing at me for being some dumb model who thought she was all that. But I wanted to be known for more than just my face and my tits and my ass. I wanted to be a musician.

I'm in the Band

While I was still modeling at car shows, I did what a million other musicians have done before me. I put an ad in the *LA Weekly* and tried to form a band. But it was really hard. Number one, I was a chick. Number two, I was a hot chick. Number three, I wasn't the typical Goth-looking, punk-rock-dressing rocker chick. I was blond. I was a model.

Finally, I got tired of everyone dissing me. So I broke it down for the last guy who called. I was like, "Look, motherfucker, I'm a model. But so fucking what, okay? I'm hot, but so what? I'm a really good musician. I can do this. And, I promise you, I'm going to be famous one day."

Finally, the guy goes, "Well, not to sound cocky or anything, but I'm pretty hot, too." So that's how I knew, awesome, he's the one.

I called my band Beyond Betty Jean, and I wrote all the songs. I loved it. I didn't care about getting a record label, or having a hit, or any of that other bullshit. I felt like, for once, I'm doing what I want to do. I'm in a band, and I get to write and sing. And who gives a shit if it's any good? I'm doing it.

Our first show was at the Cat Club on Sunset Strip in Hollywood. I'll always remember how amazing it felt to see my band name on the marquee outside. It was our first gig in Los Angeles! And it was on Sunset Strip! Next to the Whisky! It wasn't at the Whisky, not yet. But it was NEXT to the Whisky. I was like, wow, I'm living the dream, man.

Twenty Artists Who Inspired Me

1	Madonna	11	Biggie Smalls
2	The Cure	12	Lil' Kim
3	Michael Jackson	13	Pixies
4	Yeah Yeah Yeahs	14	Mazzy Star
5	Babes in Toyland	15	Sex Pistols
6	Le Tigre	16	The Clash
7	Radiohead	17	Killing Joke
8	David Bowie	18	My Bloody Valentine
9	Smashing Pumpkins	19	DJ Screw
10	Tupac	20	The Ramones

I'm Not Your Barbie, Bitch

The modeling was great for getting attention and fans. But no one would take my music seriously because of it. They all thought they knew something about how smart I was (or wasn't) just because I looked hot in a bikini. Fuck that!

I knew that you have to make sacrifices for the things you want the most in life. Music was making me jack shit for money, but I loved it. Modeling was keeping me in food and money, but it was also holding me back. So I gave myself a Mohawk. I quit modeling and I changed my website so it was no longer a modeling site. It was my way of saying, "Look, I'll show you! I don't care what you think. I just care about my music."

I was seriously broke as a joke. But I felt great. I had stood up for who I really was and forced people to take me seriously as an artist, and not just think of me as a model.

The only problem was, I kept getting hired to model, only this time, for punk-rock magazines. So I was like, "Fuck it. If modeling keeps coming to me, no matter what I look like, then it must be for a reason." I stopped doing girlie, glam stuff, but kept at it.

Sucking Dick for a Bentley

I was broke. I was sending money back to my family in Texas **AND** taking care of a friend from Sweden who was crashing with me. It was embarrassing, because I was already known as this starlet on MySpace. It costs money to keep up an image, to have new clothes and makeup, to get your hair done. I was like, "Shit, what am I going to do?"

So I'll come clean. There were times I used what I had to get what I wanted. In LA, there are plenty of guys who like to spoil a pretty girl. I drew on the help of a few special friends. But once I got to where I was going, it was, "Thanks, guys, peace out."

Believe me, they knew the drill. This is fucking Hollywood, man. It happens every day. You've just got to be smart about it, ladies. None of this sucking dick for a dollar bullshit. If you're going to do it, I'm talking about sucking dick for a Bentley. Seriously. Know your worth and make sure you get paid. And, most important, never forget why you're doing it. For me, it was all about making my music happen.

And no, you don't have to resort to having guys pay for your shit. But you do have to sacrifice sometimes. I'm just saying that it's okay, as long as you're making it happen.

That's the real secret to success. The harder you have to fight to get there, the better it feels when you do. So, no matter how bad it might be in your life right now, remember, it's only going to make it that much more amazing when you get to the other side. Just stay true to yourself. And use the venom from the haters to propel you. You'll get there.

I know it can be hard and scary. But you can get past them, just like I did. Don't let anyone tell you that you're not good enough, or you're the wrong race, gender, or sexuality. Because what the fuck do they know? Only you know who you are and what you can do. And me? I always knew I'd make it someday, no matter what anyone said. It was all I ever wanted. Well, that and true love, but that's another chapter.

Break On Through

Once I got my website going, I realized, wow, I should utilize this fan base. So, when I was twenty-two, I started my own clothing line, *TILA FASHION*, because girls were always asking about the clothes in my photo shoots, and I made a lot of them myself.

I did everything myself back then. I created all the styles and designs. I set up the trademarks. I did a model search on MySpace and set up a photo shoot. And then, once it launched, I literally filled something like thirty orders a day, *FROM MY HOUSE*. People didn't realize it, but it was Tila Tequila who actually packaged the box, taped it, weighed it, and took it to the post office.

One day, my cell phone rings, and it's a girl calling about her order. I was like, "Holy shit." Somehow, when I was filling out the paperwork, I put my phone number down as the business phone because I didn't know what I was doing!

I started getting complaints because I couldn't get the orders out fast enough. I realized I couldn't keep up, so I gave everyone their money back. But it worked out in the end. Somebody saw how hard I was working and said, "You know, there're companies that actually do all of that for you." I was like, "Really? Where?!" I didn't know any better. So I got some help, and I still have my clothing line up on my website today.

Getting Paid

When the first batch of money came in from my fashion line, I decided to treat myself. So I put down $10,000 and bought myself a brand-new '05 Mercedes convertible. All my friends were like twenty, twenty-two, still living with Mom and Dad, and here I was driving around town in this hot new car. I felt like, "Damn, I fucking did it."

I would look at that car every day, just thinking about what I had come up from and how anything's possible. It kept me hustling, too. After I shut the clothing line down, I kept working it because now I had this car to pay for and a loft downtown, where I worked.

So I made my own calendar. I set up the photo shoots, put it all together, and I sold

it online. That was really stressful, too. So, finally, I hired a personal assistant. I was twenty-two years old. I had a hot-ass Mercedes and a personal assistant.

I worked really hard to brand myself, and I kept expanding my empire. Next, I made posters and packaged deals, which were like the calendars, the posters, 8x10s, and you got a free T-shirt. I was making a lot of money, for being that young, and there were no percentages because I was doing it all myself. So I finally hired some people to help me.

It's All About the Music

I put the rest of the money into studio time. I made some friends from Sweden, and they were like, "Why don't you come to Sweden and record?" So I went for a month or two, and I was writing songs, recording, writing songs, every day. I was crashing in the basement of a friend's apartment, and I'd stay up until dawn, just writing lyrics and melodies. It was my first chance to really write and put it out there and prove myself.

So I got to be in a real studio for the first time, with these artists who were signed to Virgin Records. They helped me record my songs. I was writing with these big, experienced producers. Well, they were big producers for my world at the time.

I did a cover of "No Woman, No Cry." I put it up on MySpace, and everybody loved it. They wanted more. My next song was called "Playboy Central," which was really raw. It told this story of how, "Look, I'm playing you. You're not playing me." That was my whole thing. And people loved it. Of course, as always, there were some haters. But, as I've already said, "Who the fuck cares?"

Right around that time, MySpace blew up. I already had all of this stuff going on online. So I was really ready to hit it hard.

What I cared about was getting my music out to people. MySpace back then was just a regular HTML site, with no music players, no nothing. So I posted my music and videos on my website and put the player up on my MySpace page, so people could check it out. They went nuts for it. And everyone was like, "How did you do that?"

So Tom, being smart, saw how much people loved being able to listen to my music, and he decided they should have the same features on the rest of the site. I started that. Not bad for some dumb model, right? If I was a dude, they'd be calling me an Internet mogul.

Living It Up

Once I started to make it, it was surreal. Growing up in Texas, I used to daydream about *Playboy* and hanging out at the mansion. Next thing I knew, I was like, "Wow, I'm a *Playboy* model at the Playboy Mansion. I just met Hugh Hefner and a bazillion other celebrities."

And then I got some little things on TV. In 2003, I was a contestant on the show *Surviving Nugent.* Talk about making sacrifices to get somewhere! No, it was fun. And I started getting mad press. I was on the cover of *Stuff* magazine in 2006, and that was insane. I had worked so hard, and to see it pay off was just amazing. I got my first movie role in *I Now Pronounce You Chuck and Larry,* which came out in 2007. It was just a small part. But I was like, "That's **ME!** On the screen! With a speaking role!"

I had my own real-life *Pretty Woman* moment at a Prada store in Hawaii. This was before my show, and this bitch who worked there didn't like the look of me, so she tried to tell me the store had a dress code. I was like, "**WOW**. That's a slap in the fucking face." I decided

to show her. I tried on these boots that cost like $1,000. And, Jesus Christ, when I was a little girl, I would have been like, "Are you crazy?" But I looked at that woman and said, "Thanks. I'll take them." She didn't say a word. It felt so good, you know, like "Don't fucking judge me." And I had earned every penny of that money myself.

A Shot at Love

It's such bullshit when people say I'm a fake bisexual. The only reason MTV even approached me about doing my show was because everyone in the underground scene already knew that I'm bisexual because I spill *EVERYTHING* in my blogs.

I actually turned down my show at first, and a bunch of other offers. I thought the show could be really exploitive and bad for me. But I also knew it could really help people, because there was nothing out there about being bisexual. I guess it was a little of both in the end.

I want my real fans to know that the crazy Girls Gone Wild chick on the show, that's not me. It was frustrating as hell. But I know how much it did for me, so I'm not complaining. I can only hope it helped other people in the gay community. I mean, hello, California just lifted the ban on gay marriage. I know, none of you seem to believe me when I say this, but I really think that decision has a lot to do with my show. I don't care what anyone says. And I just saw a show on Nickelodeon where these high school students were bisexual, and they even kissed. That's so amazing!

That's not the only reason I'm glad I did the show. Believe it or not, I was actually looking for real love. I still am. And I had to break down my walls for the first time in my life. I know, I know, it's a crazy way to do it. But I did it during the first season, and I learned that I am capable of love. And I am willing to be vulnerable in order to find it. I consider that revelation to be one of the biggest accomplishments of my life so far.

October 17, 2006 1:18 PM
I LOVE U TILA

October 17, 2006 1:20 PM
this is a bomb ass pic you look absolut'.
beautiful

gorgeous.

Stunning;-)

ober 29, 2006

Photos and collage by Kristin Burns

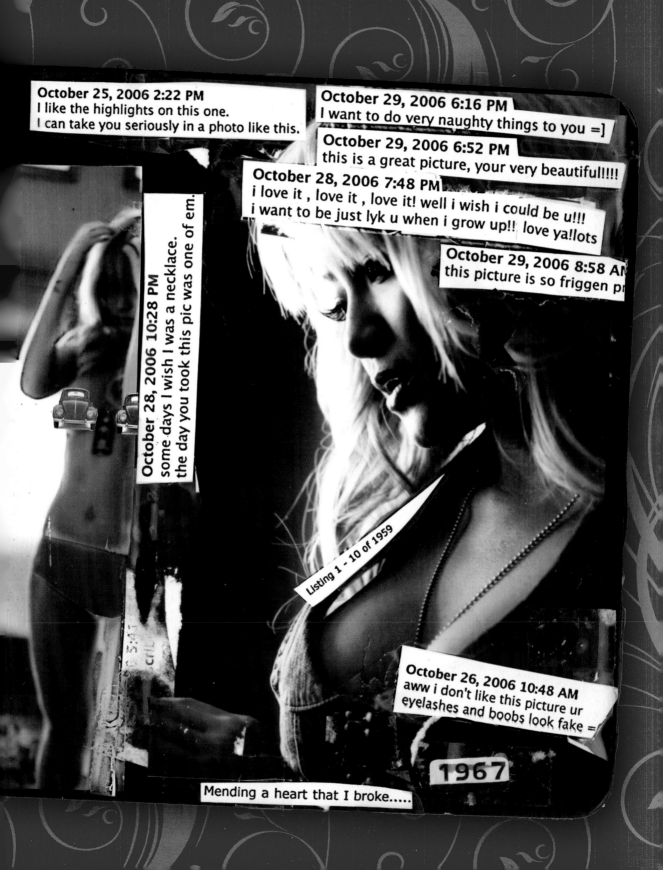

Chapter Five:
I Know What Boys Like

I've told plenty of people to suck my dick in my life. *NO*, I'm not really a dude. That's just me when I'm mad. But I have definitely played the *DUDE* role many times in a chick-on-chick relationship. And I know the guys wouldn't admit it, but I've even played the *DUDE* role in a fair share of my hetero relationships, too. Not only that, but I've hung out with dudes my whole life. I can think like a dude. And that means I can explain to you ladies why guys do what they do, and how you can deal with them better, so your relationships are a lot happier. Maybe you dudes will even learn something, too!

Ladies, have you ever wondered why guys just don't get it sometimes? Why, even if you ask them, over and over, to put the toilet seat down, they just can't seem to do it?? Or why don't they race to the phone after your first night of mind-blowing sex??? And what is it about video games that's so much more important than you????

It's no mystery. Guys don't like to be told what to do, any more than anyone else does. Sometimes they're just looking to hook up, and that night of sex was nothing more. And, even when they do like you, sometimes they don't know how to say it, so they don't call. And video games? That's left over from their caveman gene pool. But that doesn't mean they don't deserve time to hang out by themselves and do guy stuff. So here's what you need to know to land a man (and not just any lame-o) and make him happy so he'll stay.

Let's admit something right up front. No matter who you are or what you look like, believe me, there will always be someone out there that is a bazillion times hotter than you! So stop wasting your time feeling insecure about what you don't have, and start being proud of what you do! Own that shit like a fucking hooker on a good night! Walk the walk, talk the talk, and have confidence in yourself. Guys *LOVE* that!

Don't believe anything else people tell you. Seriously, guys *LOVE* a strong, confident woman! That's good news. Because strong and confident is something any girl can be.

Let's say you walk into a party that just happens to be attended by a who's who of serious A-list hotties. We're talking Gisele Bündchen, Adriana Lima, and Alessandra Ambrosio. They're all there, standing around looking as fabulous as can be.

Who gives a shit? Really. Don't go slink away into a corner. Just own it! Know that these bitches may look a million times better than you, but guess what??? *YOU'RE* the one with the attitude and spunk! That is what draws the crowd to you! Hey, it's always worked for me! I'm half the size of these ladies, but I've got twice the attitude. At least.

I mean, granted, I would fuck any one of those hot bitches at any given moment, and I'm sure all the guys in attendance would, too. I mean, duh. Hot people make for hot sex.

But would I want to have a real relationship with them? Let me put it this way. Do I enjoy talking to my vibrator, no matter how much pleasure it might give me between the sheets? Hell no! Get the fuck out of my house and don't forget your $3,000 pumps!

Top Five Male Celebrity Crushes	
1	Clive Owen
2	Wentworth Miller
3	James McAvoy
4	Ed Norton
5	Johnny Depp

Back to my original point. Every guy *LOVES* a fun, approachable girl! I'm talking about girls who are cute because of their personality . . . I'm serious! Looks do count, in that you've got to be put together. And you can't be stumbling around, acting like a big, drunk-ass mess, falling out of your stilettos.

But beyond that, guys don't really care if you look like a model. I mean, do most GUYS look like models? Hell no. And anyhow, they love a girl they can feel comfortable with, a girl who can hang like she's one of the boys. So get over your insecurities and start thinking like you can have any guy in the room. Because you can. And anyhow, everyone in that room has insecurities, **ESPECIALLY** these hot bitches, because they've never learned how to have a personality! Believe me. I've met a million girls like that.

This is where you have the advantage, ladies! **USE** your personality! Laugh, smile, dance. It's okay to get a little aggressive even. Draw all the attention toward you, and act like you don't have a care in the world! Believe me, you will generate some action!

Like, check this out, when I was at the Maxim Hot 100 List party, I wasn't the hottest girl there, physically, because there were all these beautiful, tall blondes, brunettes, whatever, with these big-ass tits. But even the friend I was with was like, "Holy shit." Because everybody gravitated toward me. I was just like, ME? But then I realized, **YEAH, ME**! Why? I'm approachable, and I'm smiling, having fun, instead of just standing there in the corner, posing with a drink. Maybe that's good to look at. But guys are like, ugh, too much work.

Here's How to Own It

There's a real art to flirting. I know because I had to learn it. Growing up, guys never asked me out. I used to be like, "What the fuck is wrong with me?" I knew I wasn't ugly. But I'd go up to these guys in middle school and I'd be like, "Hey, you're cute. Do you want to be my boyfriend?" And they'd never want to talk to me. Then, weeks later, they'd be dating some like random chick. And I was like, "What's wrong with me?"

Looking back, I can see I was being **WAY** too aggressive. The more they backed up, the more I was in their face. "Like, come on, I want to be your girlfriend. What the fuck is your problem?" Boys at that age weren't ready for such a confident girl. And men aren't all that different. They like confident women, yes, but they also like to be in charge.

So, even though I go for what I want, I'm very demure. And instead of being so bold, I let them know I'm interested by flirting *A LOT*. The best is to use your eyes. If you see someone across the room that you like, make eye contact. Not just like, "Did he see me?" And then, if he looks at you, you pretend you weren't looking at him. That ruins it.

Use your eyes to pull him in like a magnet. Give a little flirty smile that's innocent and sweet. Because guys want to fuck a slut in bed, but the girl they want to keep is the nice girl they can take home to Mom. Be both, but don't show him your sex kitten right away.

Guys love a happy, smiling girl. Don't come across as so stuck-up or hard to get. Once you get his attention, I'm sure he'll come over. . . . If you seem approachable and fun, he'll be totally hot for you. If you like him, smile and laugh, even if his jokes aren't funny. And if not, be like "Dude, go fuck yourself." No, you don't have to say that. *I WOULD*, but you can just move on, find another guy, and start from the top.

The Real Path to a Dude's Heart

Okay, once you get the one you want, here's the *BEST* secret weapon I can give you. Hold off on having sex. I know, I know, it's pretty fucking hard not to get your panties wet when you're hanging out with the dude you've been eyeing for so long. But trust me, ladies, if you want to hold on to him in the long run, hold off on sex for as longgggggg as possible!

If you make him wait, he will travel to the end of the world just to snag that punanee of yours! Make him work for that shit. But here's the key, you've got to let him know it's worth working for! Give him a little taste, *BUT NOT TOO MUCH*, of what a tigress you can be in bed! Let him fantasize about you, all day and all night, imagining how amazing it would be just to have sex with you!! Keep him drooling! Do this, and I promise you, nothing and no one will satisfy his hunger except you!

However, in order for this to work, it is *VERY* important that you actually know what you're doing in bed. If you make a man wait that long, when it comes time to hit it, you'd better be a damn maestro in bed, okay? *OWN THAT SHIT!* Ride him like a cowboy and let it allllll out! Don't be shy, *LET IT ALL OUT!* Scream like you never have before! Get crazy! Fuck like a porno star!

That is AFTER holding off on sex for as long as possible! The longer you wait, the better the chance that you'll keep him around and have him fall in love with you! And no, I'm not talking about waiting a few days! For instance, I once made a guy wait three months before he could have sex with me! Yes, it was hard at first, but after a while, it was actually a lot of fun. All we did was make out, all day long, and the passion just grew and grew, because he knew I wasn't going to have sex until the time was right . . . so we had all-day foreplay and these HOT make-out sessions that ended up being *BETTER* than the sex in the end! It was pretty intense!

And sure enough, once we got to know each other, we fell in love! So my point is, if you actually want this guy to be your man, make him work for your goods. Make him earn it.

Otherwise . . . if you don't care about this dude and you just want a booty call, just hit it and split it that night. Fuck him, and then *BOUNCE!* Guys love that! Don't stick around all night long, cuddling and talking about your life's goals and dreams. Just get in and out. Yep, pretty easy, huh? You will leave him drooling for more.

The One That Got Away

What if you're like, "I tried this, and it didn't work. He totally stopped calling me"? I know you're going to want to call him and say, "I'm ready to fuck you now. In fact, I would have fucked you on the first night. That fucking bitch Tila told me not to."

Don't cave. Of course it hurts to get rejected. I mean, I've personally made someone wait between one and three months, and sometimes it worked, and sometimes it didn't. But the times when it didn't, I felt like that's his loss, you know? You have to know that you're worth more than what you can do between the sheets. And the truth is, if that's all he's looking for, he's probably out banging other chicks anyhow. You have to elevate yourself above that, respect yourself, and really believe that he wasn't the one for you. And even if you'd had sex with him, it wouldn't have changed anything.

There Are No Rules

I admit it. In certain situations, I've had sex on the first date, and it did end up developing into something amazing. The sex was so good that the guy was like, "Holy shit! You're fucking awesome." It can work. But if you do have sex on the first date, it will have to be the best EVER. And, even more important, for the guy to keep coming back, you've got to maintain your confidence. Don't be all like, "So now that we've done it, are you going to call me tomorrow? Are we going to hang out? Do you *LOVE* me?"

Don't be clingy or needy. But after a while, if you end up liking this guy, and he really likes you, it's important to stop that game of being too unavailable. There's a balance. All of these bullshit games are necessary in the beginning, but when you really do like a person, it's important to let them know. Or else they'll think they're just your booty call, or get mixed messages and end up going away. So, when it's time, let them feel that you really do like them. It's just that you're busy. You've got your own life to live.

It's not cool to be needy and just right away be like, "Oh my God, I love you." It's best to be independent and do your own thing, while letting the other person know, "Look, I have my own life but I happen to love you, too." When you become codependent, and it's just like, "You are my life," it's like, "Ugh, please."

The Thrill of the Chase

Guys love the chase. They really do. This is frustrating, because all of a sudden, three months in, you're like, "Okay, so he likes me now because I'm this huge challenge. And once I give in to him, then what?" The game totally changes. But you can't think like that. Eventually, you just have to let down your guard. Of course, there are no guarantees. But if he splits, as long as you stayed true to yourself, you won't have any regrets. He'll be the one looking back, thinking, "This girl really loved me. I'm such a douche bag."

Sex Isn't Everything

I know, I sound like I'm talking crazy talk, right? Again, this is only if you want to have a relationship with someone. If you do, you've got to relax and just be yourself. If the guy likes to be around you, then he's going to keep calling, right? It sounds obvious. But so many ladies forget this because they get all uptight and insecure and forget how totally unattractive it is.

So what is hot in terms of personality? If you're out on a date and you're nervous, just smile. He'll think you're relaxed, and maybe you'll even fool yourself. If you're giggling—not like a bimbo, but like a cool, confident girl—it makes him think, "Wow, this girl's bubbly and fun. She's not so nervous and serious." It's a great way to break the ice.

All guys want to feel like they're funny and special. If you make him feel this way when he's around you, he'll totally call you. Be the girl who makes him feel like, "Wow, every time I'm with her, I make her laugh, and she makes me feel good about myself."

Once you've snagged him, and you two have been hanging out for a while, unfortunately, there's always the stage when he no longer notices you in lingerie and plays video games all day long with his boys.

88

What the hell happened??? Who is this loser??? Is this the man you couldn't keep your hands off and finally fell in love with? It sure is. And guess what, ladies? It's no big deal. A dude has got to have some time to be a dude.

Now, this has **NOTHING** to do with you, so don't let your feelings get all banged out of shape. Sometimes dudes can be sooo aloof. And most of the time, they don't even realize half the things they do that piss you off!

To us, this ignorance is no excuse. But it's just a guy being a guy. Give him his space to do his **GUY** things with his friends, or else he will feel like you're taking away his manhood. If you smother him, you will slowly start to drive him away because you are no longer that **COOL CHICK** or **ONE OF THE BOYS**. You know?

You have to maintain that balance. Stay sexy, strong, and confident. Lay down your rules and stand up for what you want in the relationship, but at the same time, remember to understand that a man will always be a man, and create balance between what he wants and what you want. There are just some things in life that a man is bound to do.

So, unless he is cheating on you, or you catch him jerking off to a Victoria's Secret catalog, I say, cut the guy some slack. Give him some space. He will really appreciate it, and he'll think to himself, "Wow, I have the coolest girlfriend in the whole world!"

October 26, 2006 3:15 PM
You BREAK MY HEART everytime
I think I might NEVER MEET YOU

Photos and collage by Kristin Burns

Chapter Six:
Girls Get Real

If God gave me a choice before I was born and asked me if I wanted to be a male or a female, I wouldn't be able to answer right away. I would say, "God, let me think it over. I'll get back to you in about a month or so!" I know that sounds pretty ballsy, telling God to take a chill pill. But I mean it with all due respect, and come on, that's a hard question.

Being a woman has a *LOT* of advantages, like we get to exist in these soft, sexy bodies, and we're in touch with our feelings and how to communicate them, and we have the most amazing, depths-of-your-soul connections with the other women in our lives. However, being a dude is so much easier sometimes. Don't even disagree. Let me explain.

Women have to deal with uncontrollable emotional outbursts, otherwise known as that little demon called PMS. (Don't laugh, dudes, it's a real thing!) Not to mention feeling way too deeply about stuff that's not even worth worrying about most of the time.

We get scrutinized way more for our weight. And, I hate to admit it, but we also seem to age a lot worse than men do. People always say that men are like wine; they get better with age. Well, what the fuck do we get??? A bunch of Botox offers in our junk mail?

On top of that, we have to deal with other females being catty toward one another because, well, sometimes when girls get insecure, they are just straight-up bitches. It's as though it's in our blood to be overly dramatic. Women always seem to be so jealous and needy, too, and some of them can be really conniving.

Dudes are a lot different. They're so chill. They don't hate on other dudes. Have you noticed that? In my personal opinion, it's because dudes have less shit to worry about, so they don't think about much more than bonding with one another and checking out hot chicks. Hence the term "Bros before hos!" If they do have insecurities, they hide them.

When I go out to a club or a party, there is **ALWAYS** at least one girl who says something bitchy to me, for no reason, other than just being a hater. Guys, well, they just don't go out to a club and say, "OMG! Did you see Bob? I can't believe what he's wearing! He's such a slut! OMG! Bob is such an attention whore! Let's go and like pretend to spill our drinks on him and laugh!"

Umm . . . no. Guys don't waste their energy talking smack about each other, especially if they don't even know the other dude. So my question is, "Why do females have the tendency to hate on each other so much?"

I think a lot of it isn't really our fault. Over the years, we've been conditioned to turn against each other by a world that's run by men. But that doesn't let us off the hook. In fact, I'm calling us out: We need to cut the crap right now! Yes, I am talking to all the ladies out there, straight, bisexual, and lesbian!

We have to start sticking together and standing up for one another, instead of backstabbing each other. I don't care if she's wearing that new dress you wanted to buy, or if she smiled at your boyfriend. Grow up! We get enough shit as it is, just being born a female. Why must we add more problems to our lives when they can easily be avoided?!

For instance, there's this TV show, maybe you've heard of it because it was like, not really that popular at all . . . hehe. Anyway, it's my TV show, and it's called *A Shot at Love with Tila Tequila*. Holy shit, have I gotten a whole fucking mess of new haters since that show first aired!

You would think that, being the first person **EVER** on TV to finally address bisexuality in a real way, I would be praised, at least by people who aren't total close-minded bigots! I'm not the first bisexual, gay, or lesbian person out there. And I'm not saying I'm the perfect spokesperson for the entire gay rights movement, but at least I had the fucking guts to put out a show like this, and to talk about something that has been hush-hush for so long!

But what do I get instead? I get bashed and criticized! Not only from the straights, but, surprisingly, from the lesbian and gay community as well. I mean, what the hell? I should at least be recognized for standing up for what I believe in and helping others to "come out," as I did.

First, I was mad at the haters. Then, I got mad at our culture. I realized, "Holy shit, if I was a dude, I would get praised for having a healthy libido and an active sex life. Hell, I'd get a high-five for each and every piece of ass I bagged, guy or girl."

I mean, Flavor Flav treats women like pieces of meat on *Flavor of Love.* But, yeah, he gets props for being *FLAVOR FLAAAAAAV!* And don't even get me started on Brett Michaels and his show, *Rock of Love*! Do I ever hear people bashing on him? Calling him a *SLUT* or a *WHORE*, or any of the nasty names I've been called? Nope. Because he's a man. So people think he's a stud.

I mean, look at Hugh Hefner. The man is a legend. He is a serial dater who dates like a hundred girls at the same time, and they're all young enough to be his daughter, or worse, young enough to be his granddaughter!!!!! But does anybody call Hugh a *SLUT* or *WHORE? HELL NO!* He is the king, baby! Helllll yeah . . . that's my boy, yo! Ohhhhhh shit, Hugh Hefner, that man is a pimmmmp, yo! Shit, son! Yeaaaaaaah!

Umm, yeah, okay. If I were to have fifteen boyfriends at the same time, would I be as hot shit as these men are? I think we all know the answer, so I'll leave it at that.

At the end of the day, it comes down to something so simple, yet so complicated. I am a *WOMAN*. On top of that, I am a woman with looks *AND* a brain. I just don't get why that's such a threat to people. It's just too much to handle, isn't it??? Women with brains should be some type of nun, or work at the library, or look like Hillary Clinton. If you're pretty, then you must be dumb, or a slut who uses her looks to get her way, right???

I hope you're starting to see my point, ladies. We need to stick up for one another and stop letting the men tell us how little we're worth and how we need to behave. Yes, I know, this sounds like some feminist shit, but guess what??? *IT IS!* So deal with it and start being more pro-active about how you treat yourself and your fellow ladies.

We're lucky that we have the opportunity to stand up for ourselves. If we were living a few centuries ago, I would be burned at the stake for talking like this. Or have my head chopped off. Either way, I would have been dead. Just like Joan of Arc and Anne Boleyn. Or I would have been degraded, like the rightful Queen, Catherine of Aragon! But I'm still alive, bitches, so I can fight back more than ever!

I know this chapter is **WAY** different from the guys chapter, but there's a reason for that. Guys are so much simpler and easier to understand. They're just, how can I put this nicely? They're just guys. It's easy and fun with guys. Ladies, however . . . I expect a lot more from you. You are smarter than that!

I know you're up for the fight. So here's our mission: Start sticking together and stop being such bitches to one another and blaming other girls for your own insecurities.

I hate chicks who fight other chicks over a dude!!! Seriously! Rise above that! If your guy is the one checking out another girl, or initiating the flirting, don't try to rip out her extensions! Blame him! He's the douche bag!

Ahhh, just talking about this is making me frustrated! Being a girl can be so tough! We are complex: sensitive, emotional, loving, nurturing, and often totally misunderstood. But at the end of the day, we are the ones in charge of bringing life into this world. God gave us that gift; only we women can ever experience such a beautiful blessing. **WOW!** That is magic, isn't it? And it's a good reason for women to behave with more self-respect, receive more respect from our culture, and learn to really love one another . . . even if it means you have to turn into a lesbian! Because there's nothing wrong with that!

Okay, that's enough lecture. Now, get inspired and take a little advice from me.

One woman who rocks both beauty and brains is Pamela Anderson. Everybody tries to play her down as this dumb, big-titted blonde. But she's smart. She figured that out a *LONG* time ago. She uses this misconception to get what she wants. She actually said that one of the best things about being a blonde is that when she finishes a complete sentence, people think she's a genius. She's got the gist of how to rock balance; she's a hot, smart woman who's active in PETA and has a clue about what she's doing.

Angelina Jolie is amazing, too. She is the world's sexiest woman, but no one can talk trash about her. Why? Because she's smart. You've got to love her. I mean, with that whole situation with Jennifer Aniston and Brad Pitt, if that had been any other woman, she would have been this home wrecker, this whore, this slut. It would have been poor, sweet Jennifer. But Angelina overcame that difficult situation because she's such a respected woman. She's so strong, and she's a humanitarian. You can't touch her.

I don't know why guys feel so threatened by the beauty-brains combo. They always say, "No, really, we want a smart girl!" And I think they really do. But sometimes, when it comes down to it, they worry, "How can I keep up? How can I compare?"

And other women definitely see it as a threat, because they're all like, "Whatever, bitch. You ain't all that." So it's like how do we win? The only place where we can win is with gay guys. They're like, "You are fierce!"

If only straight guys and straight girls could get it, too.

R-E-S-P-E-C-T

All right, ladies, part of stepping it up a notch is gaining more respect in this world. I don't think you have to walk around like a fucking nun or a saint. I'm definitely not perfect. But there's a time and a place to enjoy yourself. And even then, there's a way to still carry yourself like a lady. You're not out there, totally trashed and no class. Instead, you stay true to yourself. And if you want people to see you as a smart, sexy woman, then ask yourself what do you think is smart and sexy? And be that.

Top Five Female Celebrity Crushes

1 **Angelina Jolie**

2 **Natalie Portman**

3 **Scarlett Johansson**

4 **Christina Ricci**

5 **Adriana Lima**

Pleasing the Ladies

There's no easy advice here. I can tell you one thing, though. Girls like guys who don't come across all macho and egotistical, and all, like, "Hey, what's up, baby?" And no, we don't like catcalls. For the guys who think it's hot, or that we like it when they're like slapping us on the ass, going, "Damn, nice ass"—that's disgusting. Go rent some porn and jerk yourself off, because you're never going to get a real woman.

If you're a guy (or a girl), and you're into a girl, make sure you give her lots of attention. And compliments. If you go out somewhere, and you see lots of hot chicks around, does it hurt you to give her a compliment, just so she feels like, okay, my lover loves me, even though there are all of these beautiful women around? Girls can be insecure. That explains the cattiness. Say something nice about how your girl looks. It'll go a long way.

Ladies are very complex creatures. We are emotional. We are a little bit overly dramatic. Sometimes we do things we don't mean to, because we just can't help it. If guys understand that, then they're halfway home. No matter how crazy we get, just sit back and go,

"You know, my girl is dramatic. She's a chick. That's just how it is."

We want to connect with you, and talking is how we do it. If you care about us, you're going to have to sit through it. You don't have to say anything back. Don't try to defend yourself. Just listen. After we get it out, we'll feel a thousand times closer to you.

Sometimes girls want to talk about stuff that's off-limits, like your ex-girlfriend. Don't get angry. Just ask yourself, where is this coming from? Apparently she's bringing it up because she loves you a lot, and she feels insecure, and wants to make sure you love her as much as she loves you. Let her know, "Look, this girl is an ex for a reason. I'm with you because I want to be with you, because I love you." Give her the reasons why and tell her, "If you really love me and believe our relationship is real, then don't bring that up anymore." She just wants to know you're not going to leave her and go back to your ex.

The Rules of the Road

My rule is like, look, I'll call somebody at **MOST** twice. And that's it. I'd cut it off at one call, but there are technical difficulties with phones and text messages, and sometimes it doesn't go through. After the second time, if you don't hear back from this guy, let it go. If you keep calling after that, it's kind of pathetic. Because he's definitely gotten your message now. If he

didn't get the first one, he has the second one. It's his choice whether he wants to call you back or not, so don't keep fucking calling him and being needy. He has a life of his own, and you should have a life, too.

Just like guys, girls also need their girls' night out. And believe me, we are talking about you! So you'd better make a good impression. If you love her, be sure to be nice to her friends. You want them all to swoon over you as well and be like, "Oh my gosh, dreamboat!" Be a gentleman and be sweet to all their friends and family. Because these things matter to girls. It's like, "Oh, my family and all my friends love him! This is great!" Even if you're thinking "I can't stand these bitches," just pretend. It will go far.

Lady Love

One of the reasons girls date other girls is there's just this easier connection, like I explained earlier, and we understand that we're emotional. We don't have to have a conversation, like guys and girls do, about how we need to have the **CONVERSATION** about this relationship, because we know we're already having the conversation with every word we say. We feel a level

of comfort and trust immediately, as opposed to being with a guy and feeling like, "Oh, I don't know how I should act, and I don't know when I should call. I don't know if I'm coming on too strong." With another girl, it's like you can be as honest as you want and not worry about freaking her out.

Me, personally, when I'm with a girl, I play the guy role. I lavish her and spoil her with attention, because I know that's what I would want. But sometimes, because I'm not a guy, when I do want to feel like a woman, and I don't want to have so much power all the time, then it's nice to go back to a guy. That's when I get to be really girly and cute.

Sometimes girls get tired of dealing with guys being all tough and macho, and all of a sudden they find themselves being into other chicks. And they're like, "Oh my God, what is happening to me?" Nothing is happening to you. You're following your heart.

I know it's new, and it can be scary. You don't know where it's headed, or if you're straight, or gay, or what. But just follow your heart. Like any relationship, things will work out, or they won't. But if you stay true to yourself, and who you are and what you want, then you won't have any regrets. You **WILL** regret it if you don't at least try.

And if you're worried about what everyone will think, it's like, well, this is your life. Who says you have to parade around with a big sign that says I'm a lesbian? Or I'm gay? You can just tell the people who are closest to you. And if they really love you, they shouldn't have a problem with it. This isn't the 1800s, remember?

My First Time

From a young age, I'd had crushes and experimented with girls. But the first girl I really fell in love with was something else altogether. We were best friends for about a year before anything happened. She had her boyfriends, and I had my guys, and then we'd come back together and be like, "Guys are fucking stupid!"

We realized that we had so much fun together. Two days passed when we didn't see each other, and she went out and bought me a card that was like, "I miss you." And I was like, "I miss you, too. It's so weird. It's only been two days!" And then we stayed up all night, just hanging out. The sun came up, and she had this look on her face like she was really thinking about something. She looked almost kind of sad. I said, "What's wrong? Wait, you're falling in love with me, aren't you?" She started to cry and said, "Yeah, I am."

It was her first time. I had been with girls before, but I had never been this in love before either. She was scared, and I was a little scared, too. She was my best friend, and I didn't want to screw that up. We took it slow. And for a long time we didn't tell anyone. I just felt like this was mine. And it was really special.

A lot of people started asking us if we were dating. We were like, "No, we're just friends." But everyone could tell, because we were intimate in a different way.

It was one of the most beautiful relationships I've ever had. I learned so much about myself, and how much I can love a person, and what I'd be willing to do for love. Unfortunately, it didn't work out. But I'll always have a place for her in my heart. And whether it's with a man or with a woman, and whether it lasts or not, it's still *LOVE*.

so hot!!! You are so hot!!! You are so hot!!! You are so hot!!! You are so hot!!! You are so hot!!! You are so hot!!! You are so hot!!! You are so hot!!! You are so hot!!! You are so hot!!! You are so hot!!! You are so hot!!! You are so hot!!! You are so hot!!! You are s... You are so hot!!! You are so hot!!! You are so hot!!! You are so hot!!! You are so hot!!! You are so hot!!! Y... You are so hot!!! You are so hot!!! You are so hot!!! You are so hot!!! You are so hot!!! You are s... so hot!!! You are so hot!!! You are so hot!!! You are so hot!!! You are so hot!!! You are s... You are so hot!!!

Photos and collage by Kristin Burns

Chapter Seven:
Relationships

If anyone should suck at relationships, it's me. I mean, how the hell do you know what love means when you've never experienced it from your family? So, yeah, my childhood kind of messed me up. In my heart, I knew I wanted love, but it was hard for me to admit it to myself or anyone else because I was afraid to trust people.

Bootcamp for the Heart

Doing my show made me deal with my issues, and **QUICK**. Let me tell you, my feelings were NOT fake! At least not the first season. Imagine the worst heartbreak you could ever have in a single relationship, but experiencing that intensity with many relationships all at once, while allowing people to watch you, and pick at you. Hell yeah, it was hard. It almost killed me. But in the end, as they say of those kinds of experiences, it made me stronger.

It also taught me that I'm a romantic, and I'm actually **WAY** more loving than I thought. Growing up, I had to condition myself to be so tough, and to fight everyone off, and to be all like, "I don't give a fuck!" It was to the point where I didn't realize that I had so much love inside of me because I'd repressed it for so many years. So no matter what else came out of it, and how much hate I had to weather as a result, I'm glad I did the show. It feels good to know how much I care for people. And I'm not too tough to admit it!

A Real Honest-to-God Bisexual

I can't believe I'm even wasting my time on this. But if I'm going to talk about relationships, I've got to tackle it right up front. No, I am not some fake, porno bisexual who just makes out with girls to get attention or make guys hot. As I've already said, the reason MTV even asked me to do the show was that I've always been very open about my life and my sexuality on the Internet. Believe me, it was no secret that I liked girls!

I am a very sexual person, but that doesn't mean it's all about Girls Gone Wild and being stupid and flashing your tits for some crappy plastic jewels. That's how I feel like I've

been portrayed since the show. And that's why I've stopped talking about who, or how, or why I fuck someone or fall in love. It's so stupid! I mean, you don't see straight stars being interviewed about whether or not they're really straight. "So my whole life I've been *TOTALLY* straight. And it's so fun! Like I had this date with this guy, and I'm *STRAIGHT!* And I'm going to get married and have kids because I'm *STRAIGHT!* Like being straight is so cool." That's how it feels. It's like I'm bisexual. *SO WHAT?!*

Okay, now that I've gotten that bullshit out of the way, even though I know it won't be the last I fucking hear of it, let's not waste any more energy on such nonsense. Let's get to the *GOOD STUFF*. Here are some tips for making your relationships hot and happy.

Be Yourself

I know it sounds bullshit and obvious. But it's so true. Sometimes both guys and girls try too hard, or pretend to be something they're not. It's such a turnoff! Who says you have to be some slick, macho dude, or some airhead bimbo anyhow? It's actually okay to be yourself! Maybe you're a little shy, or nervous, and you say or do something stupid. That's actually kind of cute. It's a lot more endearing than somebody who's trying way too hard to be tough or sexy. Overdoing it is not being confident. It's just annoying.

You Can't Fake It

I've never pretended to be something I'm not with my music, or my personality as an artist. And sometimes it's cost me. People in the industry might decide, well, then you're not the kind of person we want to work with, and that's hard to take. The same thing can happen with relationships. You have to learn to see it as a blessing. If you try to change me, or make me into this other person, then it's like, hey, well, I guess we're not made for each other then, are we? I guess I'd better go find someone else who gets me.

Live and Let Live

You might have this initial chemistry with someone, and be like, "They're so hot!" But then you get past the whole butterflies and making-out phase, and you realize there are some things about the person that you don't like. It's **NOT** okay to change them, unless you're just helping them to be more confident and make their dreams come true. Other than that, you'd

better like them for who they are, or let them find someone who does.

Like me, for example, I'm really high-strung. I talk really fast. I get a little bit excited when I speak. I'm passionate. I have a temper sometimes. You can't just come in here and say, "You know what? You should start speaking calmly all the time and try to be quieter." Someone actually tried to do that once. Let's just say it didn't last very long. It never works. So don't even bother. Everyone has the right to be loved for who they are.

Waiting for the Good Stuff

Remember when I told you that you should wait to have sex if you really like a person? Well, now that we're finally getting into the hot-and-heavy sex and relationship talk, let me remind you that waiting can actually be really wild and fun! Because, let's be honest, a good date is just an excuse to make out, right? You know, you plan it all out, watch a movie, have dinner, but then you just want to go straight back to the house, pretend to pop in a movie, and make out for five hours.

You can still do that, even if you're holding off on doing the deed. It's just like when you were a kid, and you hadn't had sex yet, so you'd hide in the closet and kiss for hours, and it was the most exciting thing ever. As an adult, we forget that feeling sometimes. We just assume we're going to have sex. It can be so blah, blah, blah, been there done that.

But when you wait, it brings back the innocence. So make out all you want. Just don't go *THERE*. Right before it gets too steamy, be like, "I'm tired. But let's hang out again."

Believe me, the tension will build, and when you finally give it up, it will be HOT.

Mixing It Up

People always want to know what I'm all about in the bedroom. I'm not about to give away ALL of my secrets. But I will tell you that role-playing is always sexy. I've been the teacher. I've been a nurse. One of my favorites is a maid. It's fun! That's the whole point of having sex; you're free to escape into this fantasy world.

How do you get someone to role-play with you? Well, don't sit there and talk about it too much. That's awkward. "Like, okay, I'll be the princess. You be the dragon." Just initiate it, and your lover will catch on. The better you are at leading the way, the better your special someone will be at taking up whatever role you want to have played.

I also think blindfolds are a lot of fun. Definitely with handcuffs.

You can never go wrong with candles. Just the smell of hot wax releases endorphins. Or just leave the TV on if you don't have candles. That's like the poor man's mood lighting! Music is always good, too. I know it definitely puts me in the mood.

A lot of girls are weird about porn. Not me. I'm always the one who's like, "You want to go rent some porn?" And the guy is always like, "*WHAT?!*" He's like, "Wow, this chick's fucking cool." And don't worry, after a while he won't want to watch the porn anyway because he's got you. I've definitely had that happen.

Personally, I don't think porn is a big deal when you're just having fun in the beginning. But ONLY if you're comfortable with it. I mean, you don't want to be in a relationship that's

all fake, do you? And after a while, that shit gets old anyhow. I used to watch it when I was seventeen, but now I'm like, "Why watch that when I can do better?"

Also, sometimes it's about how you do it. Slow it down and take your time. It's not always about fucking all fast and hard-core. Sometimes you want to change it up a little bit. Instead of banging it out and trying to get right to that climax, *GO SLOW*. It's like now you're actually being sensual. *WOW!* That feels amazing. It builds tension, too.

Opening Up

Sex is easy. Feelings are the hard part. At least for me. There's always a battle between your thoughts and your heart. How do you even know which is which? Well, before you act on anything, sit down and sort it out. Your thoughts might say, "Okay, I'm not going to call him because he might think I'm too needy." But your **HEART** is like, "I miss him so much. I want to see him."

Even though it's scary, you've got to listen to your heart. Now, I'm not talking about stalking him after the first date. But once you've gotten past the early stages, you've got to be real with him. Because my whole thing is, if you're going to do something, give it your all. And if you really love somebody, going all out is the only way to get really close. If it doesn't work out, you'll be able to look back and say, "At least I gave it my all and there are no regrets."

You don't want to end up like, "Damn it, I love this guy so much, but he had no idea because I was always playing these dumb games and pretending I was interested in other guys and this and that." If he leaves thinking you don't care about him, you can't just pop up at the last minute and say, "But wait! I loved you this whole time."

You've got to be vulnerable and learn that vulnerability can feel good. Show him how much you care, and don't be afraid of getting hurt. Because who says it's going to go down like that, even if you've been hurt in the past? You can't think like that, or else you'll be so paranoid and scared that the relationship probably **WILL** fail.

Stay True to Yourself

There's a difference between giving someone your all and being whipped. You can show someone you really love him but still have self-respect. Because if you constantly show him love, and he's treating you like a trash bag, that's not a relationship. You need to stand up for yourself and go, "You know what? I love you, but I don't deserve this."

If you don't respect yourself, he's not going to respect you either. If you make it seem like you're always going to be around, no matter what, he'll stop valuing you. But if you show him that you love him, but he can still lose you, he won't take you for granted.

Breakups Suck

Breakups are the worst. They just are. But you can't let them flatten you. No matter how hard a breakup is, no matter how sure you are that you'll never find anyone else ever again, and that, even if you do, it's **NEVER** going to be the same, you're wrong. No matter how bad you feel now, you will heal. You will move on. There will be somebody new. There will even be somebody better. Everyone in this whole entire world goes through it. The most important thing is not to have any regrets. If you two don't end up being together forever, it's just not meant to be. There's nothing you could have done or said differently to change that. So don't beat yourself up over it. Just deal with it and move on. It hurts. But we're strong. We heal.

I've learned a lot from every relationship I've been in. That's the whole point of having relationships, and getting older and growing up—it's to learn more about who you are. And the best way to learn about yourself is to have your image reflected back at you by another person. That's how you come to know who you are, what you want to be, what you don't want to be, what mistakes you made, what you're not going to do next time. See, breakups can be good. Just make it better each time, and you'll keep getting better.

Move On Already

I know it hurts. I know it hurts like a motherfucker. But you've got to let it go. If you keep thinking about the past, you will just manifest the same things again and again in your life, and it will become a pattern. If you're like, "Oh my gosh, I'm so scared. I always end up getting hurt because I've always been hurt in the past," it'll happen. The universe is always listening.

But if you think, "I've gotten hurt in the past, but I'm going to change it this time," you totally can. I mean, look at me, I got hurt in the first season of *A Shot at Love,* and then I was like, "Oh, I don't want to do a second season. It's too much." But then I did. And even when **THAT** didn't work out, I'm still looking for love. You can't let the past affect who you want to be or how you want to live your life.

Love Yourself

Everyone always says, "You've got to love yourself before you can love or be loved by anyone else." It's so true. But what does it mean? One day I asked myself, "How the fuck do you know if you love yourself anyhow?" I can say I love myself, but what does that really mean? I'd like to think I love myself, but I'm not sure that I do. It's a process, you know? Paint a picture of the person you want to be and create that person inside of you. Work at it. You have to find your own inner happiness and stability. If you're hooking up with somebody to fill the void that's inside of yourself, you can't love him or her. But when you love yourself, you don't need anyone to make you feel better. It's just an added bonus when you're involved with somebody cool.

Last Call for Love

Now that I've been able to reach so many of my goals, this beautiful thing is happening. That whole time I was trying so hard to make it, I was hiding my heart, just working, working, working, this robotlike machine, and **NOTHING** could touch me, and **NOTHING** could fucking hurt me. And now it's like, "Oh my God, I have this huge heart, and all I want to do is **LOVE!**" All I want is love, because it's the one thing I never had. Recently, I've had love from fans. I've had love for my music and for my passions. But I've never had **REAL LOVE**. And now I'm like, "Wow, I saved the best for last. My heart. Aw."

And who have I been saving it for? Someone strong who can see all of me and be like, "WOW!" Someone who can see who I really am and not just who he or she thinks I am. Because I know I have so much to share with the person I love. I have so many things inside that I know are beautiful, but I can't reveal them unless I'm really in love. You know? I don't want to give it all away to random people. I want to build a life with someone until the day I die. That's all I want.

I know, after this book comes out, everyone's going to be writing to me like, "I can be the one. That sounds perfect! That's **ME!**" And I'm like, "Great, so now I've got to do season three. **LAST CALL** for Love with Tila Tequila. Just as long as I find it!

My Top Five Hot-and-Heavy Fantasy Hookups

1 **Anne Boleyn**

2 **Batman**

3 **The Hulk**

4 **Wonder Woman**

5 **Cleopatra**

Hardcore smokin'. Street Cruisin'. LA fo life!

Photos and collage by Kristin Burns

Chapter Eight:
Fan Questions

In the past seven years, I've gotten thousands and thousands of e-mails and MySpace posts from my fans, so I've got a pretty good handle on what you all are thinking and feeling and stressing about. Because this book is for **YOU**, the fans who helped me every step of the way, and believed in me, and backed me, and kept me company when I was struggling, I'm dedicating this book to you! And I'm giving you the chance to ask me real questions about the real problems in your lives. Just for you, I'm giving you my answers, along with my perspective on life, and all I've learned while having my heart bashed, and stomped, and kicked in along the way.

Okay, let me get this first question out of the way right up front, because I hear it **A LOT**.

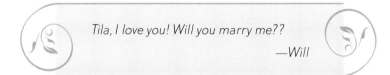

Tila, I love you! Will you marry me??
—Will

I just had to include this one because I get marriage proposals at least a thousand times a day! So it's ironic that I'm still always looking for love, right? That's how it goes.

But, in answer to your question, **NO!**

I'm sorry, boys and girls, but unless you fit the criteria for the person I want to spend the rest of my life with, don't waste my time. Here's what I'm looking for:

1   You must be strong. Not just physically strong, but mentally and emotionally fierce, too. You must make me feel safe and secure just by being around, because I know I can trust you, and I know that if anything bad happens, you will always be there to back me up and support me. You will fight for me, as I will fight for you. Just like Bonnie and Clyde. That's my dream relationship! Well, not the whole killing spree part, but just how passionate they were about each other. It should be *YOU AND ME* against the whole world, baby! Not you and me against each other! I can only love a strong motherfucker! Cuz I am a tough cookie myself!

2   You must already love yourself. That may sound weird. But if you don't love yourself, how can you ever love me? You can't be an empty person, and only think you love me because you don't love yourself, and you want love from me to fill that void. You'll just be this insanely needy human being, and that annoys the hell out of me! Cut it out! Go be single for a while and learn to love yourself! Once you have achieved that, you can hope to find a happy, healthy relationship . . . then, and only then, you can give me a call!

3   You must be able to stand on your own and have excellent style! Sometimes being in the entertainment field requires socializing at important events. A person who is not well put together and does not have good style is such a turnoff! I mean, you don't always have to put on a Dior gown or a Prada suit, but you do *NEED* a keen fashion sense. There is always a way to have style, even if you're on a budget! I can't be walking the red carpets of this world next to some douche!

4   You must be ambitious! I'm a hardworking gal, and the slightest sign of laziness turns me off sooooooo much! It's like, "Get your fucking ass up off the couch and go find something you're passionate about, or get the fuck out of my house!!! If you're just going to mope around, hoping money will fall from the sky, you need a reality check, or maybe you need me to smack the shit out of you until you wake up!" Ughhhhh. I have met so many lazy people in my life. And freeloaders! There is *NOTHING* worse than freeloaders! Lazy bums are going nowhere fast, and I don't need them in my life

to bring me down after I've worked so hard! Sure, if you are truly happy being a slacker, then I am happy for you. But if all you do is complain about how much you hate your job, but you're not going out there and grabbing life by the balls, then you're just like every other schmuck who's wasting his or her life away! Get the fuck out! I hate lazy people!

5   **SEX!** Seriously. I am very sexual. When I am in a relationship, the sex had better be damn good! If it's not, the relationship won't last. I can guarantee it! Sex is one of the main ways I release my emotions and passions. Sometimes it's even like therapy after a stressful day! You have to have a **VERY** strong sex

drive and not be inhibited **AT ALL** with me. Sometimes I will want to have sex with you up to five times a day, at the very least! I like passion. I like deep kisses. I am very loud in bed, so you'd better not be afraid of the neighbors hearing. And I assure you, they will. Believe it or not, someone actually called the police on a former flame and me because I was screaming so loud! People thought I was getting killed, or something, so they called the cops! I am an animal in bed, and you need to be able to keep up. If that scares you, then you're not for me. The more I love you, the better the sex will be! *winks*

6 You'd better have a brain, too! I love an intelligent person who can keep up with me in conversation. I am very sarcastic, and I have a big sense of humor! You've got to be able to match my incredibly sharp wit and come back with something just as funny! I get so turned on when a person gets my jokes and can actually beat me at my own game. That's how I know you have a brain. Then we can have a brain bang!

7 If you are sweet and sensitive, you'll score *MAJOR* points with me. As tough as I can sometimes seem, I actually have a *HUGE* heart, and I love being in love! I love to love. I love how love makes me feel. I love sharing that amazing feeling of being in love with the person I love! Have I said the word "love" too many times? It's not possible! Someone sensitive will bring out even more of these loving sides in me. Be sweet to me. Show me how much I mean to you. Tell me exactly how you feel. Don't think twice about texting me ten times a day just to tell me that you miss me, or you're thinking of me, or you love me. That will never get old to me. I hate games, and I adore honesty. The

more you open up to me, the more you will be rewarded with my boundless loyalty and passion. I will go to the end of the world for you! Not to mention spoiling the hell out of you every time I step out of the house. I can't help it. When I am in love, I just want to spoil my lover with lavish gifts, trips out of town, and everything that I always wanted but never got from others in my life. Yes, whoever gets me will be one lucky person!

Tila,

How did you come out to your family, and how did they take it? It's something I haven't done yet, but I've known I'm bisexual for almost five years now. Thanks.

—xlaidtorestx

Hi xlaidtorestx,

It's definitely not something that's easy to do. I had a television show that forced me to tell my parents. That didn't necessarily make it any easier. It's just that I had to do it, or else they were going to find out, along with millions of other TV viewers, the first night my show aired.

It's always a bit scary, because you're telling them something personal, and you don't know how they'll react. I know I felt awkward when I made the call to tell my parents. My friends had always known, and my siblings had always known, but my mom and dad had no idea. They come from a traditional Vietnamese background, which means they had totally different rules and values growing up.

I think it's best to do it sooner rather than later, because then they won't have the added

hardship of feeling betrayed that you kept it from them for so long. And you will seriously feel this heavy weight lifted from you when you do tell them.

If you're feeling really overwhelmed, instead of sitting down with the whole family and being like, "Hey, everybody, I have an announcement," maybe start off with just your mom. Have a little mom time and be like, "Hey, Mom, you know I've had boyfriends. Well, I just wanted you to know that I've had girlfriends, too. You know I love you guys so much. I just wanted to let you guys know this because you're my family, and I hope you don't feel any different about me because I'm still your same loving daughter."

Maybe your mom can help you tell your dad and the rest of your family. Having her on your side can make it easier for everyone to accept it, and it will probably go a lot smoother than just making an announcement at the family reunion, like, "Hey, Grandma, guess what?!"

And remember, they love you. They're your parents. They'll support you. Even if it's a shock to them at first, they'll get used to it. If they don't respond well, maybe have them watch my show to see that it's no big deal. Or try to get them to go to a support group. The most important thing is that you feel free to be who you are and enjoy your life without judgment or grief from anyone else, even if they are your family.

Hey Tila!

Is it okay to pick fights with your boyfriend, just because you want the attention? Is it wrong to ask your boyfriend about his ex-girlfriend, like sex-wise? Do you think it's okay for your boyfriend to go to a strip club and get a private lap dance?

—Anonymous

Hey Anonymous,

Let's take this one question at a time. Alright, I fully admit it. I've picked a fight to get my guy's (or girl's) attention without even realizing I was doing it. But no, it's not okay. What's the best-case scenario? You finally get his attention, but it's not in the way you want, because now you're fighting, and he's all pissed off. Maybe he even ends up walking out the door. If it happens one too many times, he might decide he can't deal with this relationship anymore. Then you'll be feeling full-on regret. You just wanted more of his attention, but now he's gone, and you don't have **ANY** of his attention.

Back it up and ask yourself why you want his attention in the first place. Is he spending all of his time watching sports on TV? Is he too busy hanging with his boys to hang with you?

If so, go back to my chapter "I Know What Boys Like" and school yourself about how guys tick and how to keep them happy. I hate to break it to you, but he deserves some time to himself. It's not about you 24/7. But this is a relationship, right? If he's continually not paying any attention to you, okay, there's something wrong. But don't pick a fight. Don't try to get his attention by making him jealous, or sticking your Sidekick in his face and showing him how some other dude is blowing you up. Instead, try sitting down with him and saying, "Look, I really want to feel close to you right now. I want to be able to talk with you and spend some time with you." Or, even better, if you just want to love him, jump on his lap, start kissing him, nibbling on his ear, and kissing his neck. I'm sure you'll get his attention then, but in a **VERY** good way!

Alright, moving on to question number two. Hell, yeah, it's wrong. First of all, if it's his ex-girlfriend, that's what it is, his ex. She's out of his life for a reason. Maybe he dumped her because she kept trying to do things to get his attention! Leave the exes out of it, as hard as it may sometimes be. I mean, what's the point in comparing yourself to his ex anyhow? The fact is, they're over. You need to focus on what you have instead. If you keep on about your insecurities, and the ex, and what the sex was like with the ex, it's only going to create a whole mess of problems. Who wants to hang out with somebody who's all twisted with insecurities and constantly fighting with him about his ex? I guarantee you're just pushing him away. So never talk about the ex, or sex with the ex. Focus on your own sex life, and everyone will be a lot happier (and more satisfied).

And finally, question number three. First of all, it depends on who you are. I have friends who have a special type of relationship, where they're cool, and they trust each other, and it's totally no big deal for the guy to hit a strip club. Sometimes the girl might even want to go along because she thinks it's hot. If that's the dynamic of your relationship, sure, that's great, and it is hot. But if you, personally, don't feel like it's right for him to go to a strip club, and you feel like it's disrespectful to you, then, no, it's not right. And you should tell him, "Look, why do you need to go? It fucking kills me. It's disrespectful. Do you really feel the need to jeopardize our relationship by getting a twenty-dollar lap dance?" Break it down for him, and he should respect you and cut it out. Maybe you can even spice things up and give him a lap dance at home. Then everyone will be happy.

Hi Tila,

My partner and I have been together for nine years now. The first two years were wonderful, but then something happened. Out of the blue, she told me that she wasn't a sexual person, and our physical relationship came to a stop right then. Since that happened, we only make love maybe once or twice a year. It kills me, and I don't know what to do. She is bipolar, and I don't know if that has anything to do with it or not. I suffer from acute depression, and after a month or so, I start feeling so unwanted. Right now, I feel like we are just two friends sharing the responsibility of raising our daughter. Am I wrong to feel this way? I don't want to cause more problems between us, but I'm running out of options. I finally told her the other night how I felt, and she did the same thing she always does: She says she loves me and will try to change. Is it wrong for me to want her, knowing that she feels the way she does? What can I do to make our situation better for all of us, especially our five-year-old daughter?

Thank you,
Want the Best for My Daughter

Hi Want the Best for My Daughter,

This is a tough one. I'm not inside your relationship, and I don't want to disrespect anyone, but it sounds like she may be seeing someone else. If the first two years are amazing, and then, all of a sudden, out of the blue, she's not feeling sexual anymore, and you're only having sex twice a year, my first thought is that she's out messing around with someone else. Now, don't do anything until you know for sure it's true, especially as you've got a daughter to consider. But I personally feel very strongly that those are signs of somebody who's really drifting away from the relationship. And even if she's not, it's so unhealthy for both of you to try to stay together just for your daughter's sake.

This relationship is probably making you more depressed than you need to be. And even if she is bipolar, the fact that you're making excuses for her behavior instead of making sure she's getting the help she needs is not healthy either. You can try saying something along the lines of, "Look, honey, I love you. I'm really sexual, and I need to have sex. We need to talk about this." But if you even have to bring up the fact that you need to have sex, and you've

been together for that long, it's not good. Your sex life should already just be rolling. And if she's not reciprocating, and she's the one who says she's not sexual anymore, and you're saying you are, you two need to get clear on the fact that you are in different places and want different things. You need to split up and do your own thing for a while, whatever that means for both of you. Maybe find sex with someone else, or start dating other people, because hanging on to something that's so unhealthy is just going to make it worse. And the longer you hang on, the worse it will get. Nothing is going to change until you have the courage to make a serious change.

Most important, the problems in your relationship are having an impact on your daughter. And your daughter should be your number one priority. I know it's hard, but it would be better to separate for a while, so that your daughter is not in the middle of your depression and problems. Take some time apart, and really take a good, hard look at your relationship. If you both still love each other, then try to work it out. But if your daughter is the only reason you are staying together, that's not good enough. It's better for her to see that Mommy is happy, even if that means she's on her own.

> Tila,
>
> I have a question. My girlfriend of more than a year and a half is joining the army, which means we will have to hide our relationship from everyone for four years. Tila, I have never hid any part of myself from anyone. I strongly believe in being who you are. So my question is do you think I should stay with her? Don't get me wrong, I am one hundred percent in love with this girl, but we would not be able to go out in public as a couple or even tell our friends and family. So do you think it would be worth it?
>
> —Don't Want to Hide

Hi Don't Want to Hide,

Okay, you're thinking too far ahead. You're digging this hole by thinking, "You're going into the army, and we'll have to hide for four years." It's like, step back! You're in today. Four years is not until four years from now. Take it every single day at a time. Don't think too far ahead, because that's when you get too overwhelmed, and you start getting bogged down by negative thoughts. Just see how it goes instead.

That way, you don't have to cut it off so drastically. At least give it a chance before you decide to break it off. While you're hiding it, you might realize, "Oh, hey, this isn't so bad. It's actually okay. I'm glad I didn't give up on it."

But if it does get really hard, and things just don't work out because of the distance and time apart, then you'll at least know, "Hey, we gave it our best shot."

Don't wimp out on a relationship just because you're afraid of what the future brings, because you never know what's going to happen. If you're optimistic about things, anything is possible.

As far as hiding goes, I do agree that you shouldn't have to hide who you are. I also really believe that a lot has changed in this day and age, and that a lot will continue to change about peoples' attitudes regarding sexuality. So, for now, just take it easy, go with the flow, and I think everything should be cool. Don't think too far ahead. Just focus on the fact that "I love this girl, and we're doing really well right now."

Hey Girl!

We've all seen how far some people are willing to go to get your attention (via your hit show A Shot at Love*) . . . I want to know . . . what's the craziest thing YOU have EVER done for love???*

Much respect . . . always.

Joanne

Hi Joanne,

Well, I'm crazy already, and when you combine my craziness with love, there is no stopping me! The craziest thing I've ever done for love? There are so many to choose from. I turned down almost $200,000, because I felt like I'd rather just be happy and spend time with the person I loved, as opposed to being away a lot for work. I know that sounds nuts, but sometimes you have to trust, well, this is what makes me happy right now. Before the show, I gave up a chance to be in the Hollywood spotlight even more than I am now. I almost jeopardized my career, my well-being, and my life, just for someone. I take a lot of risks in my life, and that goes for my love life as well.

I've never been the one who's like, "I'll change my whole life for you. I'll fucking eat this shit for you." But I have changed who I am for love. And that's saying a lot. Because I'm very stubborn when it comes to who I am and what I represent. But sometimes you have to make compromises to show your love. I've done a lot of crazy stuff, but it's always been to help the other person see his or her potential in life and be a better person. That's how I love someone. Love is a selfless act. It's not selfish. I give a lot.

I've definitely taken my lovers on these surprise getaway trips, first class all the way, baby. And I give all kinds of gifts. There's no limit to my love, and what I will do to show it. I always try to protect the one I'm with from people who might bad-mouth him or take advantage of her. I'm the protector. I can be a little aggressive, but that's how passionate I am. But at the same time, I'm not whipped. Not even close!

Hi Tila,

What do you think about love when there's an age difference of twenty-three years? I have been divorced for three years now, and I have a girlfriend (who is thirty-two). I'm in love with her, and she says that she is in love with me. Sex is fantastic! She thinks I'm Superman (ha)! We've been together for four years (I was separated for two years before I got divorced). We never fight, we're always laughing, always having fun. But age is always on my mind. What will happen twenty years from now? She will be fifty-two, and I will be seventy-five. Should I worry about this? Do you think age matters? I ask you this because you are young, too. What would you do if you were my girlfriend? Do you think this relationship has a future? Or should I forget about the future and enjoy the moment?

—Bboydad

Hey dude,

First of all, snap the fuck out of it. You should be so thankful and happy that you're fifty-five years old and have a young woman who is madly in love with you. Even more than that, you should be ecstatic that you've been with her for four years. I haven't **EVER** been with anyone for longer than a year! So I admire the fact that you can even have such a happy, healthy relationship for so long. You should enjoy the moment and stop worrying about what's going to happen twenty years from now. If you keep worrying, she's going to have to keep reassuring you, and reassuring you. And, in the end, you're just going to manifest her leaving you because you didn't focus on enjoying what you have now. And besides, let's break it down. Twenty years from now, when you're seventy-five, she won't be no spring chicken either. She'll be fifty-two.

I can also tell you that, as a woman, I can understand why a young girl might go for a much older man. She probably feels like young guys may stray. They don't appreciate her as much as they should because they think they're young, and they can get any chick they want. But with an older man, she feels like, "Okay, this man loves me, and he's not going to leave me for someone else." She probably likes the security of knowing that her man and her relationship are solid.

I mean, look at Catherine Zeta-Jones and Michael Douglas. He's an old fart, and she's a young, gorgeous lady. You might wonder, "What is going on?" But she's probably so sick of younger guys, or guys her age, who mistreat her, or don't appreciate her. And here comes this older guy, who's been through it and knows that he just loves her. And for that reason, they're married, they're happy. And he doesn't worry about losing her.

I think you should be thankful, enjoy the moment, and know in your heart that you will get married and be together forever. It sounds like she is very much in love with you. I wish you and your lady the best. See, there are some happy endings! Hell, to be honest, I wish I had something like that.

Tila,

You're a very sexual person, and I, too, consider myself to be very sexual. You're also famous, as am I, on a much lower scale. I sing with a band. I really want to find love, as I believe you do, too, but nobody takes me seriously because everyone automatically wants just my body . . . a.k.a. sex. I love sex and am very open to anything, but I want to find true love, respect, and trust, and that needs to come before the sex. I guess my question would be: Having made it obvious that you're a very sexual person, how can you be taken seriously in order to find true love and respect? I'm tired of being alone.

—¢ ¾ Judy ¢ ¾

Hey Judy,

I covered this in "I Know What Boys Like" because it's a real problem. But there is an easy solution. I swear. So, okay, we are sexual beings, and people don't take us seriously. They think we're easy. We have to force them to acknowledge our personality.

If you really want to find true love, here's what you have to do. It used to be, I'd jump on my impulses, and it was always just dating, and sex, and nothing serious. But the minute I decided, look, I want to have a real relationship, I made the guy I was dating wait three months before I would fuck him. He gained so much respect for me and fell madly in love with me.

Not at first. He came on all strong and tried to sleep with me on the first night. But I held off. After three days of hanging out, and of him trying to get some, he finally stopped. We got to know each other. We hung out, watched movies, and talked. We talked a lot. He got to know me as a person, and that sexual image slowly faded. In the end, I found someone I could have a relationship with who really loved and respected me.

So, if you want that, too, start out by finding someone you really like, or a guy you think is cool, and get him to take you out. Then, make him wait for you as long as you possibly can.

I'm not saying just a week or two weeks either. I'm saying, if you can, try to wait a month. I know it ain't easy. But that's how you can overcome your sexual image and have someone take you seriously. Because the guy will be like, "Damn, this bitch is hot. But, damn, she's not as easy as I thought she would be." As he fights for you, and spends time with you, he'll realize he's totally in love with you.

And if he doesn't? Then he's a damn fool. Because you're amazing and sexy and cool, and he was lucky to have you. I mean it. You just have to tell yourself that you did your best, and be happy that you know your worth. If he wasn't into what a strong, self-confident woman you are, then fuck him. He can go fuck all of those dirty, herpes-having, band groupie girls, while you hold out for your dream man. You will find him. Plus, being true to yourself feels good, regardless of what else happens.

Hi Tila,

When you've had enough with your man, and you can't go through any more drama because you've had it, how do you really let go and move on? It's like, you want to move on, but he always keeps walking back into your life, and you just can't let go, but in your heart, you really want to let go because the relationship is turning sour.

Thanks,
—Crissy8156

Hey Crissy8156,

I can relate to this question. It's hard to let go. But you've got to. People hang on for the wrong reasons, because they don't want to admit it's not good anymore. At least you have the balls to recognize that this relationship is turning sour. It sounds like he's not letting you go. I'll bet he's even being all sweet, and crying, and making you feel guilty.

This is seriously bad for you. So here's what you do. Don't cut him off, just like that, but sit him down and have a **BIG** conversation where you throw down, in the nicest possible way, all the reasons why your relationship doesn't make you happy anymore. You can even tell him that maybe you'll get back together someday, if it's meant to be, after you've had some time apart. But, for right now, be clear about the fact that you have to break it off. And then, stick to it. Stop hanging on for the wrong reasons. It may have been great in the beginning, but things change, people change, and it sounds like it's anything but great now.

And then, be fierce. Don't answer his calls. Don't return his e-mails. Try your best to avoid him at all costs. Cut your heart and mind off from that situation completely, so you can give yourself enough space to heal and gain perspective. You never know, maybe in two months you'll realize how much you miss him, and maybe you can build a new relationship, from scratch, that's healthy and good. But you've got to make a clean break first. Seriously, do not make contact for as long as you can. Not even as friends. Not even in that pretend way we all do, like, "Hey, we're cool. Let's go to lunch." That doesn't work. There's no change until there's really a change. I know it's hard, but I've been through this same shit. For two months we were back and forth, explaining this and that. But finally I decided I needed to cut this shit out. I let him go, and I just focused on my work. It hurt, but really, it felt so much better. It was definitely the right thing to do.

You have to totally cut yourself off from him for long enough that you don't feel like you have the right to ask him what he's up to. And then, if you see him, and you're really reacquainting yourselves again, maybe a new relationship could work out for you. But it's not likely after it's gone sour. And believe me, you're really, truly better off without him. There's something called a life out there, you know? So do it. People forget that.

134

Tila,

I'm in love with this one girl, and she loves me back. But she wanted to take a break in the relationship because of the distance, and because we never get to kick it. So I agreed because I thought it was best for her. Then, the next thing I know, she has a boyfriend. We still flirt and talk about getting back together. But every time I ask when, she says she doesn't know. She ignores my phone calls, messages, and IMs all the time. But she always tells me, whenever we do talk, that she is still madly in love with me. What do I make of this? What should I do?

Love always,
Emo Kid

Oh, Emo Kid.

I hate to harsh on your fantasy, but I have to break it down for you. She has a boyfriend now. It sounds like she's stringing you along because you still love her and she likes the attention. Maybe she does love you. I can't say what's on her mind. But look at it this way. You're long-distance. You broke up because of the distance. She has a new boyfriend now, and she still talks to you and flirts with you. These are all bad signs. I mean, think about it. Is it really going to work out? Even if you get back together, then what? Are you going to move there? Is she going to move to be with you?

Instead of worrying about all of that, **YOU** move on and do your own thing for a while. Let her do her thing. Don't worry about when you're going to get back together. Maybe, after a while of being apart, you'll both want it enough that you'll be able to deal with the long-distance thing, and it will work out. But for now, stop focusing on her and her boyfriend. You need to have your own life.

And seriously, even if you do win her back, how will you know she's not cheating on you with the other guy? You'd be better off finding someone in your own area code.

Tila,

When two people are totally different, kind of Beauty and the Geek, should love be pursued? I mean, even if there is an attraction (though odd) between the two, wouldn't the relationship not last long because they're so different? Sometimes it's hard not caring about people's opinions and what they might have to say about your life. What if you loved someone who wasn't as socially graceful as you? Would you risk being talked about in order to go out with him and give him a chance?

—Vee

Hi Vee,

First of all, if you really love this person, you'll tell everyone to back the fuck up and respect your boyfriend. And you'll be clear on the fact that you love him and you don't care what they think. They don't know him like you do. They don't know all the qualities that are amazing about him, so why do you care what they think anyhow?

If you're going to be all superficial, and worry about what people think, then maybe you should go find yourself a rich, preppy boy who treats your ass like shit and dumps you for another fucking bimbo with big tits. You make the call. I mean, seriously, I don't want to be harsh, but you've got this great guy who loves you. Do you know how many people would kill for that?! Hell, **I'D** kill for that! And here you are, worrying about whether or not your friends think he's a geek? Maybe he's the one who's too good for you.

Tila,

Do you believe in love at first sight? If so, how do you know that it's true love?

—Danielle

Hey Danielle,

I absolutely believe in love at first sight. I've felt it. You don't know why, or where it comes from, but you just feel it, and so does the other person. You can't explain it, except to say it's magic. So that must be what it is. Plus a good dose of chemistry, and maybe even a meeting of your souls. Maybe they have encountered each other before in a previous life, so when you see each other, you get this almost familiar feeling. Your heart doesn't lie. So you just know, okay, this happened for a reason. And yeah, it's true love.

Because how do you know if anything is ever true love? You don't know. You can only know that, in that moment, wow, it feels like love at first sight. Beyond that, don't question it. It's a blessing. Not everyone gets to experience it. Maybe it won't last forever. Maybe it will! No matter what, it's still magical. Don't be afraid.

I wish I had love at first sight every day. It could go away at the end of the day, and then tomorrow, I'd have something new. I love that feeling so much!

Hey Tila,

My question is, How do you know if what you're feeling is real? Like how do you know if you're really in love?

—Ericka

Hi Ericka,

You just know. Block out what your mind is telling you, and ask your heart what you feel. And if your heart responds in a positive way, where you feel butterflies and get all excited every time you're around that person or you think about that person, go with that feeling. Don't overanalyze it. If you think too much, it becomes this kind of unhealthy, super-uptight relationship, where you're watching the other person's every move to see if it's real, or if you even trust this person. Who wants a relationship like that? If this person makes you feel good, that's all that matters. Real or not, live in the moment, and enjoy it.

Tila,

My question is about relationships. How can you tell if a girl is uncomfortable on a date, or if she is not into you?

Much Love!
LiiMiiTeDWiiDiiT,
b4ysh1t510

Hi b4ysh1t510,

Well, let's say you meet somebody, and you think, "Great, let's go on a date." If you're wondering if she's uncomfortable, watch to see if there's any awkwardness between the two of you, or if she's kind of quiet, or if her body language is telling you that she's not really that into you. If she's moving away from you, or she's kind of aloof, then she's definitely not interested. If she was interested, you'd know!

If a girl's interested in you, you're going to notice her giggling a lot. She's going to be laughing at everything you say. Her eyes will be gazing upon you with adoration. She might kind of play with her hair while she's talking to you. She'll be smiling a lot, and giggling. If she's doing these things, you're in. She likes you!

On the other hand, if she's not into you, she'll give you short answers, and she'll seem distracted by other things happening at the restaurant. Or she might just seem real stiff and cold. That's when it's not going well. If she's not into you, and she's not calling you back after your awkward date, or she's making up lots of excuses about why she can't see you again, you just have to accept that she wasn't right for you and let it go.

Hey Tila,

I am 15 years old, and I am having a problem with a boy. I've been going out with this boy for a year. Now it's to the point where he wants to have sex with me. What should I do? Thanks!

Much love,

Jessica

Hi Jessica,

Well, it's been a year, and I'm really proud of you for waiting that long. The fact that he's been willing to wait shows that he really loves and cares about you. But that doesn't mean you have to have sex with him right this minute. It's more important that you feel comfortable and decide it's the right thing for you. You shouldn't feel pressured in any way, just because you've been together a year, and now he feels it's time to do it.

You only get one chance at the first time, and you never get to take it back. So make sure you feel a hundred percent confident about taking it to the next level. Make sure he is the right person to share something so beautiful with. It is a special experience.

Try talking to him about it and let him know that this is really important to you. Let him know that you love him, but you want to make sure you're doing this the right way. Be sure he knows that any hesitation on your part is not because you don't love him. It's just because you know how significant this decision is. This is a big deal. It's not just like, "Hey, let's make out." It's like, "Hey, this is my virginity!" There are a lot of feelings that go along with that. It's a huge step, and you don't want to regret anything. And don't worry, when the time is right, you'll get there.

If the time isn't right, keep holding off. Wait until you're actually comfortable enough to feel ready. Because once you feel comfortable, you'll know that it's time. You'll flow into it naturally, and it'll be awesome and beautiful. If it's not at that point yet, just keep waiting. Don't let him pressure you. You'll know when it's time.

Hey Tila,

I have a question about sex. What if a guy finishes early, but the girl didn't even feel the satisfaction? What should the guy do?

—Luke

Well, Luke,

You'd better learn how to go down on a girl, and use your damn fingers, until she definitely gets her satisfaction. If you don't know how, then you'd better start practicing on her. I'm sure she won't mind! You can't just bust a nut and be like, "Okay, I'm finished. Let's watch TV." Go down on her for another hour. Whatever it takes.

Tila,

I know this might be a little too R-rated for you to answer in your book, but if you can, that would be great. What can you do to make a guy last longer? And what other interesting things have you tried when it comes to sex that you suggest we try? Thank you so much, keep doing what you are doing.

Love,
Irene

Hey Irene,

Get him some Viagra! **NO**. But you can't really tell a guy, "Look, you need to last longer." Try this, though. If you feel like he's about to cum, it's actually fun to just stop for a little bit and do some more foreplay. Maybe make out a little more, tease his body a little bit. If you stop right before he's going to cum, and then you start again, it will drive him crazy (in a **VERY** good way) and help him to last longer. It's that much more exciting for both of you, because you're not just like, bam, boom, done. The tension builds and builds, and then when he does finally cum, it's like **WOW!**

To make things interesting during sex, try to really let go. Don't be afraid to explore your deepest fantasies and let it all out. A lot of people are shy, even with their boyfriends and girlfriends, and that can take some of the pleasure out of sex. Try to get past that. Maybe try something new and exciting that you've never done before, like doing it in a place where you might get caught (just don't end up in jail!), or maybe get some toys. Blindfolds are always a turn-on. Whatever you do, just make sure to have a lot of fun with your partner, so it doesn't get boring. Put some effort into it, but without putting any pressure on anyone, because that will just make it awkward. And then, relax and enjoy!

Hey Tila,

I am just wondering, if your family doesn't support you with your career choice, what should you do? I would like to be an exotic dancer, but my family does not support me in the least. How should I go about it if I have no support?

Yours truly,

Lindsay

Hi Lindsay,

You're probably thinking, "I'm strong enough to do this. I'm not going to let people take advantage of me. This is a way to earn good money." I get it. I've been down that route. I knew that I was strong, and that I would be okay doing what I had to do to make it. So I get where you're coming from.

But I also understand how your family feels. Honestly, if I had a daughter, and she said, "Hey, Mom, I want to be a dancer," I would fucking lock her in the closet. There is nothing you can say that will make your family okay with the idea of you getting naked for guys and possibly endangering yourself in the process. Your family wants you to be safe. You should feel lucky that they care about you and think you're better than that.

I don't ever judge people, because I've been through a lot in my life, but stripping for me was a last resort. I wish I had had a family that supported me and talked me into doing something else. I hated every second of dancing and taking off my clothes. It was the most disgusting feeling I've ever had. I did it because I had these goals that meant everything to me, and I made my money, and I got out of there. But I was messed up. I thank God that I made it out alive. I wouldn't suggest anyone go through that.

I'm going to have to side with your family on this one. If you have a choice, do something else. There are lots of other ways to explore your talents. Try to get started as a model. Sign up for a dance class. Then, you can come out to LA and be one of my dancers, and we can hang out and have a lot of fun!

Hi vryxpeculiar,

Okay, first things first. I never got put down, as in people going, "She's a fucking lesbian!" But I've definitely been criticized for a lot of things, like modeling, and being in *Playboy*, and being seen with other women. I still get criticized for these kinds of stupid things every day. But what can you do? You know. They can all go suck my dick!

Next up. My family is still in Texas. I don't mention them on my show because my show has nothing to do with them. I feel like my life is already out there, but that it's my life, my show, my decision to be famous. I'm not going to jeopardize my family members' well-being by pulling them into the spotlight when it wasn't their choice. Plus, I've always been a very private person. There are some things about my life that I keep to myself, and my family is one of them. I would never put them on the show.

Yes, I have had stalkers, and it's not fun. When a person crosses that line from being a fan to a stalker, it's definitely scary. I get very upset because this person is now violating my privacy, and my rights, and putting me in a dangerous position. I've always hoped that by connecting with my fans and talking to them online every day, it really shows them how much I do care about them and their support. But some people take it too far.

Fame is weird. Sometimes I think I never want to be with another famous person again, because it's just too much with both of our lives combined. But then, sometimes, I think it's better to be with someone in the entertainment industry, because we can understand each other's lifestyles. Also, it's hard because you can never be sure what a person's intentions are, so it's a relief to be with someone who comes from the same place as you do. You know they're not using you. They have their own life and job and fame. I guess it all comes down to who the person is. Whoever is strong enough to understand that my life might be crazy, but it's just a fucking job, it's not ME, that's the person for me.

Big titties.

Photos and collage by Kristin

You are so hot!!! You are so hot!!! You are so hot!!!

Chapter Nine:
Pop Culture

My American Idols

People always ask me who my idols are. Well, growing up, it was Madonna **OF COURSE**. I admired her for her strength. She really inspired me. And our life stories are so similar. Madonna was on her own from a very young age. She went to New York City by herself when she was seventeen. And everyone told her "You **CAN'T SING!** You sound like fucking Mickey Mouse! Are you crazy?" Everyone was talking shit. They told her she wasn't good enough for anything. So she did what she had to do. She even posed nude, and then the pictures ended up in *Playboy*. All kinds of stuff happened to her, but it didn't stop her. She believed in herself so much, and was so full of conviction, that other people slowly started to believe in her, too. I loved to read about her when I was struggling, because it reminded me, look, shit happens to people. But if you believe in yourself, you'll get to where you want to be and prove everyone wrong.

The other big one for me was Tupac. I have every single Tupac magazine cover. He saved my life. When I was living in Texas, I listened to his songs over and over. He's the one who encouraged me to come to LA, you know, To **LIVE AND DIE IN LA**, that's where all the dreams are made. Just because he was out thugging and gangbanging, that doesn't matter. That's who he was. He was real. He was my role model. His music was poetry. I always felt like Tupac was my soul mate, and when he died, a part of me died. I mourned him for years and felt so alone and like, "Who's going to be my leader?" I had to make my own way and write my own songs.

Other rappers try to be like Tupac today, but they're just fake, wannabe posers. Even my lovely Madonna has jumped on the bandwagon of what's cool, I guess because there's so much pressure to stay on top. So when people ask me today, "Who do you look up to? Who are your influences?" sadly enough, there's no one.

It's a real fucking shame, too, because I can see that people are hungry for the next real thing; someone who's like Madonna was when she first came out, someone who's challenging and raw, full of life. I hear it in the letters I get from my fans every day. And I know just what they mean.

There are people I admire. But it's different now. It's not like they could save my life. They're just cool. Like Angelina Jolie. I think the reason she's one of the most beautiful women in the world is not only because of her looks—there are many gorgeous women out there who aren't half as bitching as she is—but because her beauty from within shines through. She's a good person who strives to do something with her life and give back. She has this amazing family that travels and does all kinds of cool stuff together. That's what I want to strive to do now, to have some fucking purpose in my life.

And if she can do it, I can do it, too. Because she was also a little lost when she was younger. She was also the bad girl with tattoos who had all these boyfriends and was promiscuous and wild. And it's funny, because she was twenty-six when she adopted her first son, and she started to seem so much happier, and her life turned around. And I'm twenty-six, and it's as if the same thing that happened to her is happening to me.

If you live a wild, party life, you can go one of two ways. You can either keep prancing around, getting your picture taken, soaking it up as much as you can, and not doing shit.
OR you can be like Angelina Jolie and say, "Okay, I'm in a position where I can be heard and have a lot of influence, and so I'm going to do good things and give back." I definitely want to be like Angelina Jolie.

I think J.Lo did her thing really well, too. It's like today, yeah, she's had kids and it's kind of boring and blah, blah, blah. But when she was coming up, she was hot shit. Sure, she's not that great of a singer. But she could dance, she had her ass, and she had this sexy ethnic vibe. She just had this total J.Lo brand *GOING ON*. When she came out, I was like seventeen, eighteen, and I remember being like, "J.Lo. *PLEASE*." I never wanted to admit it, but I loved her. I thought she was so pretty. And I loved her music.

Another smart person, who used to be a bad boy—see, notice a trend?—is Johnny Depp. I mean he was a rock star in Hollywood, living it up, doing all sorts of crazy shit. And then, something happened to him, and he realized, "Look, this is what I love to do. But it's just a job. There's something more important in life." And so he decided to move far away from Hollywood, so he can live his life, without paparazzi following him around. I think he's a brilliant guy. Those kinds of smart choices are why people like that are so respected in the long run. They don't get caught up in all of this pop culture bullshit.

Ed Norton is awesome, too. Something about him is just so hot. I fell in love with him when I saw him in *American History X*. Of course, I'm sure everyone did. I love his work. And there's just something about him. He's not trying to be one of *GQ*'s Men of the Year, or whatever. He's just himself, and he can be a nerd. But you can tell he's really intelligent, interesting, and mysterious. He's not like those other Hollywood douche bags out there trying to be the next sex symbol. But he's definitely a sex symbol in my world.

These people are all amazing. They're a little older, and they've had a chance to figure their shit out. Thankfully, there are a few stars coming up now who seem like they have this same kind of integrity. Natalie Portman represents the type of woman I really admire. She's been acting since she was a child, but she didn't grow up to be some messed-up child star. She's not in the tabloids. She's really got it together. She takes her job as an actress seriously, and she just started her own production company, so she can direct. She's elegant, and pretty, and smart. I really respect her as a strong young woman. Plus, she's got an amazing sense of humor. I first fell in love with her when I saw her in this *Saturday Night Live* skit, and she was rapping, and being so stupid. Her character was acting how I act. She was running around, rapping, cursing people out, being like, "Fuck you," and, "I'm hard-core." And I was like "Is that me? That's really funny!" I've been in love with her ever since.

Scarlett Johansson is another girl who is in the same age range as those young Hollywood types, but she's nothing like them. She doesn't go out and party, and get totally wasted, and do crotch shots. She's got elegance, and class, and she associates herself with elite people in the entertainment industry. People take her seriously as an actress. Not only that, but she's gorgeous, and she's voluptuous, and she doesn't have to use her sex appeal to get attention. She's respected for who she is. I really admire her, and I think she's sexy, too.

These are the people kids should be looking up to. I feel bad for them, though, because they're getting brainwashed by all these false idols. Like Britney Spears, for instance—I love Britney, don't get me wrong, but she was packaged to be a star. When she first came on the scene, everyone used to say she was the next Madonna. But that's not really true, because Britney was packaged. People told her, "Say 'I'm a virgin.'" People told her, "You don't smoke. You don't do this, and you don't do that. You're an angel. This is who you are." She wasn't allowed to think for herself. That's not like Madonna. That's not going to help anyone, like Madonna helped me.

In the end, Britney rebelled, **TOTALLY**, against the image everyone had built up, just to find herself again, and it caused a mess in her life. Kids either have that to look up to, or all of these socialites, who just run around finding ways to stay in the spotlight because they don't have any other talents.

Poor Britney. It's like, you know, damn straight she was one of the best performers in the world. She was profound onstage. But what did people say? They were like, "Oh, the bitch can't sing. She's fucking lip-synching." It's like, "Oh yeah?!" Sure, she might not have been Céline Dion or Whitney Houston, but who fucking cares? Nobody wants to hear that voice all the time. It's like, if you do, go to fucking church! You know?

It's like, yeah, those bitches can sing, but they look like fucking nuns. You know what I mean? It's like women performers aren't allowed to be sexy, and independent, and talented. It's like they're always saying, this singer who isn't as hot, **SHE'S** a **REAL** artist, **SHE'S** a musician. It's like, give me a fucking break. I mean, if they didn't have that voice, they would be nothing. And even if they are talented, why does that mean we have to compare everyone else to them? Who wants everyone to be the same anyhow?

Everyone loves to hate on Britney Spears these days. But I'm all about bringing her back. She was an entertainer. She was really good at what she did. Maybe you didn't want to admit it at the time, maybe you were like, "Whatever, she can't sing." But, let's be honest, watching her perform in her music videos, or at awards shows, it was like, **WOW**, she's really putting it out there. And I don't know if you've ever tried it, but getting up there and trying to dance like that, and sing at the same time, it's fucking hard work. And then, to go on tour, doing that every single day. I mean, these people are here to entertain you, and you fucking rip them to pieces. It's like fucking *GROW UP!*

Just look at the demise of Michael Jackson. To this day, this man is one of the most talented artists of all time. If you try to say there is not one Michael Jackson song that you like, you're a liar, and I will slap you in the face. But he's a total freak show. And I blame us, our culture. We are the ones who built him up and tore him down. Viciously.

So I'm going to change all of that and give credit where it's due. Even though Britney didn't claw her way to the top like Madonna did, she still inspired me. She still worked her ass off. And it always seems to be the ladies who get bashed on so much.

It's easy to be on the other side, and point fingers, and go, "You're a fucking slut. You suck." But it takes skills, and balls, and hard fucking work to make it as an entertainer. You can sit your ass down, working a nine-to-five job, or whatever, and talk shit about people all day long. But what these artists have to endure, I think it's incredible.

And then you have someone like Justin Timberlake who's getting all this credit. It's like, "Please, give me a fucking break." Okay, cool, I give him **SOME** credit, too. He's talented. But, you know what? I love Britney a thousand, million times more than Justin Timberfuckinglake. He's so safe. Sure, he can sing. But I just don't see the sexiness in him. I mean **SEXY'S BACK?** Who the fuck said it left? You know? Are you crazy? It's like, Jesus, give me a break. It's like **WAY** overhyped. It all goes back to my theory that it's way easier to be a guy. They can get away with murder.

And what are we left with? There's no one today who can even come close to touching Britney Spears when she was at her peak. Even Rihanna, she's not a great performer. It's like uh, "Umbrella," okay, you're fucking boring. I don't see any new pop stars who bust their ass today, who are dancing, performing, looking good, working out, just capturing the audience. I mean we have like who, Miley? What is she? She's a fucking baby. And they're already making her into the next Britney Spears anyhow. The poor girl; she's so young, and they're already tearing her down.

The adults keep creating these role models, thinking they're giving the kids something to love, but in the end, they're really just damaging them. There's no one real to look up to anymore. And these kids need someone real. They're out there, going through *REAL* life, real struggles, experimenting, fucking up sometimes, in order to find themselves, and no one is saying, yeah, that's okay. We all do that. Life's fucking messy. It's such bullshit.

> **Top Five Most Awesomest People of the Year**
>
> 1 **Natalie Portman**
>
> 2 **Scarlett Johansson**
>
> 3 **Johnny Depp**
>
> 4 **Ed Norton**
>
> 5 **Me (It's my book. I can say I'm the most awesomest person if I want to, thanks.)**

A Star Is Born

The moment that led me to where I am today happened when I was eleven years old. I was in my bedroom, sitting on this stool, looking in the mirror. I had big pin-striped pants on, believe it or not, and a white T-shirt with a black ribbon at the top to match the fucking pin-striped pants. I thought I was so cool, *AND I WAS*, okay? In that moment, something strange happened to me. I had this feeling of importance, like I was going to do something of meaning with my life. I just *KNEW* it, and no matter how fucking hard it was to make it happen, I never lost sight of that.

See, I always wanted to be famous, but I never really cared to be a celebrity. There's a difference. Along the way, my original dream somehow got confused with fame. As pop culture changed, and we all got brainwashed by *US Weekly,* I lost track of what I was really supposed to be doing. But I caught myself. I was like, "Wow, holy shit, I almost got it right, but I fell onto a different path because it was so similar to what I really wanted." I've snapped the fuck out of it now. I've realized that being a celebrity is totally different from being respected and admired by many people, which was my original goal.

I'm not above admitting that I got off track, and I'm getting myself sorted. Even today, I don't know exactly what it is I'm supposed to do. But I know it should be something of meaning and value. So now I'm going to take this chance to make it right.

High School with Better Clothes

You can't rely on fame, or popularity, or the approval of others for a foundation of love. Because people are fickle, and their approval is fleeting. It lasts for a minute, and then the next minute, they hate you, and you feel like, "Did I do something wrong?" And it's tempting to keep changing, so they'll love and accept you. But first and foremost, you have to love and accept yourself.

Once you get behind that velvet rope, you realize it's just a sad, lonely place. It's hard to find people you can trust, which is why I feel so lucky to have my fans supporting me and keeping me real. Hollywood is all about this petty bullshit: fame, backstabbing, and scandal. It's like high school. Who's more popular, and what are you wearing?

Get Real, Bitches

Even though people say I'm a pop culture icon, I'm already dreaming *A LOT* bigger. I remember, on MySpace, where they ask you to list your heroes and influences, I chose Joan of Arc, Queen Elizabeth, and Anne Boleyn—women who actually did shit. I want to be thought of like those women, like Madonna and Angelina Jolie, instead of these girls today who just stumble around causing stupid scandals and being train wrecks.

Because the attention they're chasing, it's just a temporary feeling of false grandeur. And I know that I have a higher purpose. Sure, laugh. Be all like, "Who does that bitch think she is?!" But it's true. I shouldn't have made it. I shouldn't even be alive. And the fact that I am, it gives me a purpose. What is this purpose? Well, you're reading this book, aren't you? I'm hoping it's helped you. I'm here to help my fans and anyone else I can.

Because sometimes I look back and say, "Wow, when did I become what people perceive as this freaky, bisexual, *GIRLS GONE WILD* chick, who's jumping on tables, when I am the total opposite of that?" And that's why I'm writing this book and finding new ways to express myself; I want to put the real me out into the world.

The truth is, I only just learned who this *REAL ME* is in the last few years. It was doing the first season of my show that really helped me to know myself better. I now know that I'm very empathetic toward people. I'm compassionate. I love people, and I want to help them. And believe me, this generation needs help, and there doesn't seem to be anyone else stepping up to do the job. There are no real role models for kids, and I feel like I definitely could be one. As much as some of the critics would laugh at that, at least I'm honest. I'm real. I have a voice. Nobody packaged me to be a certain way. I am who I am.

At least I'm trying to do something and be a real person. I'm not saying I'm changing the world every single day, but I feel like I'm on the right path. I'm getting there. It takes time. We're all human. We all make mistakes. See, I'm admitting it. Maybe kids can learn from my mistakes and start to get that anything worth having, or being, takes work.

DELTA 3200 PROFES

36

35A

Photos and collage by Kristin Burns

Chapter Ten: Music

People are always like, "Who the hell is Tila Tequila, and what the fuck does she do?" So I tell them I'm a musician, actress, and reality star. But I love being a musician the most.

Even before I knew I could sing, I always felt this need to express myself. Growing up, I didn't really have much of anything, but the one thing I did have was this little journal. And I **LOVED** it so much. I was eleven years old when I first started writing poetry.

I could never really talk to kids my own age because I always felt as if I was a lot older than them. I had to grow up and basically be an adult when I was still a kid, so I couldn't relate to anyone my age who still got to be a kid. So I told everything to my journal instead.

My favorite time of the day was when the sun was setting and everyone else was doing their own thing. I'd close the door to my bedroom. I'd pull out my journal and draw pictures and write poems. That was my way of escaping. My life was such a shit hole, and the only way I had to get out of it was with these creative thoughts and fantasies.

Finding My Voice

When I was around fifteen years old, I started writing music, just by joking around with my friends in the car. We listened to a lot of techno and stuff that was all instrumental. And I started making up melodies and lyrics, and we'd just laugh. But, actually, I was good. I realized that I really loved doing it and could make up good melodies to all these songs, even on the fly. Plus, I had all this poetry, which could be lyrics.

You know how people always say that music saved their life? Well, it definitely saved mine. Because I had nothing else going for me, and I had no reason to think I was anything special. But when I was by myself, I would listen to music, and it would inspire me to dream all these big dreams and write them down, along with all my poems.

It was a way to express the sides of myself that I kept hidden when I was out there building my reputation as the baddest bitch on the block. And it felt so good! I started to feel like I had this hidden talent that nobody knew about, and it was just *MINE!* I used to write about my girlfriends, boyfriends, and all my feelings. That's how I got started.

Rockin' Out Bitches!

TILA TEQUILA

162

Pure Freedom

I absolutely love anything that's one hundred percent me, like writing, or making music, or creating something. It's so pure and free. When you're in the studio writing a song, you don't think about anything else. There are no bills, no deadlines, no schedules, no personal-life drama. There's no, "Don't forget to call Mom."

You're just in the studio. It's kind of like a meditation. You get lost. Hours pass, and you don't even realize it. I never want to leave. I feel really safe in the studio. I love being there, creating new things, and once a song is done, I love listening to it and being like, "Wow, I did this. I made this." That's why I love music more than anything else.

I mean, I may not be like a Whitney Houston or Christina Aguilera, but I'm not trying to be that type of artist anyhow. Music is just something I love to do. And no matter what anyone says, I know that I'm good at it. I write all my own songs. I write all my own lyrics. I coproduce all my own music. How many other female pop culture icons can say that? Not any that I know of.

A Little o' This, a Little o' That

One of the cool things about music is that you can be so versatile. You can start with some hip-hop, and then try out a pure pop sound, and then pull in some reggae, or rock. It's like trying on new shoes. You don't want to wear the same red shoes every day. You want to try on different styles and colors and shapes and sizes. To me, that's what music is like.

I grew up in Texas listening to everything. I listened to screw music and techno, what they call drug music. But I also listened to adult contemporary, like Clay Aiken and all that old-people music. I loved everything, because each song would give me a certain unique feeling. The only thing I never listened to was country music. But I drew on everything else when I started making my own music.

A One-Woman Band

When I came to LA, I decided that I really wanted to make music, but it was just like with everything else. I was like, "How the fuck do I get started?" You know, I don't have any demos.

I don't have any money. At that time, I didn't even know how to play any instruments. I decided to get things going for myself, rather than waiting for anyone else to help me out. I bought my first guitar. I got guitar books, and I taught myself, day and night. Seeing as how I didn't have any friends out here, I had a ton of time on my hands. I started learning electric guitar, and slowly, I got better until I was really good at it.

I had a computer with a webcam, so that was my mini-studio. I'd think of a new riff, and I'd go, "Wow, that's really good." So I'd

Top Ten Songs to Get Busy To

1   "Voyage to Atlantis" by The Isley Brothers

2   "Bump and Grind (Remix)" by R. Kelly

3   "Red Light Special" by TLC

4   "Pony" by Ginuwine

5   "Pretty Girl" by Jon B

6   "Nobody" by Keith Sweat

7   "What's On Tonight" by Montell Jordan

8   "All the Things (Your Man Won't Do)" by Joe

9   "Doin' It" by LL Cool J

10   "One in a Million" by Aaliyah

turn on the webcam and record myself playing. It all overlapped into these songs, so it was like I had my own little studio.

And then I got a keyboard and a bass. I started learning how to play everything. I was like a one-man band. I even blew myself away, going, "Wow, I play bass, guitar, piano, keyboards." I knew how to work the drum machine. I bought a drum kit. I made beats.

That's how I got even more into music, just figuring out, okay, this bass line goes with this drum kick, goes with this keyboard sound, and together it makes this song. Sure, it might not have been the best song ever, but it was a start. So I was writing from the very start in LA, and then I put out ads to form a band, and Beyond Betty Jean happened.

I love making music more than anything else in the world. Even to this day, when I do my club appearances, and the DJ plays my song, I'll be right up there, singing and performing for everybody. It feels so good being out there, like, "I don't give a fuck!"

Keeping It Real

It's not always easy doing the thing you love most. When you write something from your heart, you're vulnerable. And when you put it out there, and people bash you for it, it hurts. But you've just got to be ready for that and not let it get to you. So, as long as I'm happy with

a song, and I never feel like I sold out, then I don't ever let myself feel bad when I get criticized. Instead, I say, "Well, you know what? I didn't do it for you."

Whether it's making music or doing anything else, you have to do it for yourself. You have to do it because you love it. If you start allowing other people to judge you, and you're only doing it to please them, then it's not fun anymore.

Just like I've been telling you all along, you have to stay true to yourself. And don't let them try to make you into something you're not, no matter how much pressure you get from anyone. It's like, with me, once I started to get a lot of attention on MySpace and in magazines, some people in the music industry all of a sudden got **REAL** interested in my musical career. And they had this vision of me being like the Pussycat Dolls or something really Disney. And I was like, "Are you fucking serious? Have you seen my naked pictures on the Internet? I don't know how that's going to happen."

So even though they said they had this plan to make me a big star, and there was all of this money on the line, I didn't buy into it, and I decided to keep doing it all myself. I was like, "I'm not going to be some cheesy, lip-synching pop star with these dance moves, and this little mic on my headset who's all like *ONE, TWO, THREE, ALRIGHT!*"

It's like, "Are you fucking kidding me?" I knew I couldn't do that. First of all, it's not believable. Second of all, I wouldn't have been able to keep up the charade. I've already conditioned myself to be this really independent girl, and once you've tasted freedom, there's no going back. So I didn't take any of the record deals I was offered.

Instead, I decided, "Hey, you know what? I'm going to be an independent musician. How about that?" Then I can keep writing songs with profanity in them and do whatever the fuck I want. That doesn't mean that I'm like that every day, that I'm rolling up to my mom and dad's house and being all like, "Fuck your man, Mom!"

But mouthing off and maybe having a little attitude can be a way to create different personas. And that's awesome! I'm not one of those people that's like, "I take my craft so seriously." Music, to me, should be fun. It should allow you to express yourself in different ways. And like one of my other favorite things in the world (that's right, you guessed it, **SEX!!**), music should allow you to dive into a fantasy world, to be someone else, and try different things, and not have anyone ever tell you that you're wrong.

I don't ever want it to stop being enjoyable or feel like, "Fuck, I've got to write a song that sounds like Céline Dion." Because that's not me. And it's a good thing that it's not me, too. There are plenty of other artists out there who do that. Who says their way is any better anyhow? Whitney Houston became a crackhead, so who fucking knows? I'm just going to be myself, make the music I love, and hope my fans love it, too.

Outro

Sometimes people ask me, "Is there anything you regret?" And I don't know how to answer. Sure, I have many regrets. But each one of them has only made me stronger and helped me to know myself better. And so, in the end, there's nothing I **REALLY** regret.

That's why I have the tattoo on my arm that says, "C'est la vie." It means "That's life." And that's how you have to look at it. Bad things happen. Sometimes we even cause the bad things to happen. We don't always get to have control. But we do get to choose how we react. Do we fall apart, or do we get the fuck back up and learn something from what happened, so we can do it better, and maybe even **BE** better next time? That's right!

My real message, to myself, and to all my fans, is just to keep it real. No matter what happens, or how many regrets you may have, you'll never look back, cringing and going, "I totally went along with this thing that was so **NOT** me. And I'm so embarrassed by it now." Because if you do betray who you are and what you believe in, when people start to pick on you (**AND THEY WILL**, let me fucking tell you), you won't even be able to stand up for yourself. Because deep down inside, you'll know they're right. And you'll feel like, "Wow, you're **RIGHT**. That show really was exploitive and lame. This song really is cheesy. I don't know why I did it."

BUT, if you do things from your heart, it's totally different. People can say, "Your music sucks. Your book's fucking lame." And it doesn't even touch you. It's like, "Great, you don't like it, but at least I do." Even if nobody **EVER** ends up seeing any of your work, it still feels amazing. **IF IT'S REAL**. Because if things don't make you happy, what's the fucking point?

I mean, what's the point of me fighting so hard, and doing all this, just to sell out and become someone I'm not? It's like Jesus Christ, I'd rather go back to Texas and work at Wal-Mart than do that. At least then I'd get married and have some babies. Life's too hard as it is. You can't worry about doing things just to please other people.

No matter what you do, not everyone's going to like you. But too fucking bad! At the end of the day, no matter what happens, it's okay to be who you are, even if people *DON'T* get it. So don't let anyone make you feel bad about yourself. *EVER*.

It's not easy. We live in this society where we're all taught to, like, "Go to school. Go to college. Go to grad school. Go to work for some big company." There's no room to have one single thought of your own. But what I'm saying is you *CAN* find a way to break out of that mold and be free. And if you do, that's when you really find your purpose in life. Dharma, they call it. That's when you're really doing what you were put here to do: Live life to the fullest and give back by being your true self and helping others to do the same.

You can try to fake it, but you won't be happy. And you'll know you're not really on the right path. Even when you think you're doing what you're supposed to be doing, you'll know deep down inside that it's not really your dream or who you are.

It's just hard to see any other way at first. You're scared. You want to be happy, and you're not, and you don't know why. Well, you won't ever be able to be happy if you don't take a risk on yourself and learn to trust your instincts and what your true self tells you. Because finding happiness also means taking risks, and if you keep betting on yourself, even if you fail at first, it's inevitable that you'll win eventually. Look at me.

There are a million different ways to make it happen these days. That's the best thing about this whole new breed of Internet celebrity that I've helped to create. People finally have to admit, look, times change. It's not the 1800s anymore.

Labels don't work anymore. And I honestly feel as if I had a lot to do with that, by doing everything I ever wanted to do and not letting anyone put a label on me, no matter how hard they tried. How many people can say they're a clothing designer, musician, actress, reality TV star, model, and, now, an *AUTHOR? AND* a sex kitten on top of all that? And I graduated high school. And I went to college. It's like, "I can be anything I want to be. I can be a fucking chef. I can be a mother. Not anytime soon. But someday!"

Oh, and you forgot to mention that I'm also an ex-criminal. Why don't you list slut, whore, and stripper, too? I've been many, many things. And there are many things I still want to be. I refuse to pick one thing, just so people will take me seriously. It's like, watch, I'll do it all *AND* be a humanitarian, *AND* still write songs about fuck your man!

When the haters got ahold of me, I could have easily turned into some crackhead junkie who just lost it and felt like "This sucks. This is so hard. Why are people judging me?" But I was like no fucking way. I'm so turning it around, every single day.

Now that the show is over, I want people to know that, yes, that was a part of my life, but it's not who I am 24/7. So I'm looking for things that can help me get back to just being ME again. Music is still my number one passion. So I've got an album in the works. That's the most fun because I get to be my own boss in the studio, without anybody telling me, "Write a song about being bisexual! Write a song about kissing a girl!" I'm going to write about whatever the fuck I want to write about. It's just for me and my fans.

I've still got my clothing line. There's some new stuff up on my site that I designed, and I'm looking to do more of that. I want to do a shoe line. I love stilettos, like really high, sexy shoes. I can't stand nonsexy shoes. And I'm less of a high-fashion, trendy girl, and more into just an edgy, sexy style. I think a lot of girls out there would really appreciate what I have to offer, this really sexy, badass style. So I'm doing that.

www.tilashotspot.com

I definitely want to do some movies. But not like some hottie and naughty bullshit. I want to do something that's dark and mature, like a morbid—*GEE*, what a surprise!—fucked up, really unexpected role. Something with a lot of emotion, like *Girl, Interrupted* or *Gia*. Or even an action movie, because I'm always running on such **HIGH** adrenaline. I get so bored with people, and so many things, and if something's not interesting to me, I just feel like, okay, I'm not on the right path. I want to do something that's exciting. I want to feel like I could die tomorrow. I want to shoot a movie that's so fucking crazy, a movie that explores all of my emotions and lets people see like, "Wow, this girl is really in touch with her emotions. She's really dedicated to expressing herself."

I feel weird talking about this because it's not for publicity, but I do want to do more charity work, too. Because of how I grew up, I get what it's like to be less fortunate.

And as ironic as it sounds, I am **ALWAYS** looking for love. That's one of my main goals for the future. I want to finally find the one who gets me on a level that's deeper than just Tila Tequila, the pop icon. Somebody who gets all of me, and is able to connect with me on a very real level. Because when you understand where I came from, why I am the way I am, and how I was able to overcome these things, I feel like it's solid. And if that person maybe comes from the same background, then we can understand each other even better. It's like, "Wow, sometimes we feel like it's just you and me against all of them. So fuck them! Let's just go at it like Bonnie and Clyde." To me, that's happily ever after.

And if you want to know more, you'll just have to wait until I write my autobiography. Darker, sexier, and giving up the **FULL** story of my early years, it's going to be hot. Just wait.